GOALKEEPER TRAINING MANUAL

Fundamental Drills to Improve Goalkeeping Technique

by Lorenzo Di Iorio and Ferretto Ferretti

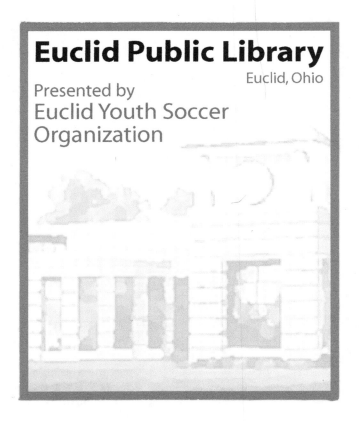

Original title
L'allenamento dei portieri - Eserciziario indispensabile per migliorare la tecnica
By Lorenzo Di Iorio and Ferretto Ferretti

Translated from Italian by
Maura Modanesi

First published 2002 by Editoriale Sport Italia Srl Milano Original title:
L'allenamento dei portieri - Eserciziario indispensabile per migliorare la tecnica

Copyright   Edizioni Correre 2002

**Library of Congress
Cataloging - in - Publication Data**

by Lorenzo Di Iorio and Ferretto Ferretti
    Goalkeeper Training Manual

ISBN No. 1-59164-082-2
Lib. of Congress Control No. 2004094654
© 2004

Editing, Layout
Bryan R. Beaver

Cover Photo
Richard Kentwell

Printed by
DATA REPRODUCTIONS
Auburn, Michigan

Reedswain Publishing
612 Pughtown Road
Spring City, PA 19475
800.331.5191
www.reedswain.com
info@reedswain.com

TABLE OF CONTENTS

"The sense of positioning", which is determined by the position of the ball on the field, is one of the most important skills for goalkeepers and provides the foundation of good goalkeeping.

In order to take up the correct position, the goalkeeper must always try to stand along the line (bisecting line) dividing in two equal parts the angle of a hypothetical triangle created by the line joining the two goal posts (the base) and the ball (the vertex of the triangle) - (see illus. 1).

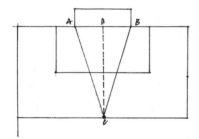

Illustration 1: If you connect the two posts (A and B) and the ball (C), you can form a triangle (ABC) whose base is the goal line and the vertex is the exact spot where the ball is positioned.
The bisecting line (DC) dividing the angle in two halves is the line along which the goalkeeper must always try to position.

This concept of positioning is valid in most cases, but there can also be some exceptions resulting from particular tactical situations that develop during the game.

For example, if there is also a defending player standing inside that hypothetical triangle - suppose he is on the goalkeeper's right side - the correct position of the goalkeeper is no longer along the bisecting line, but slightly to the left, because the defending teammate reduces the attacker's shooting angle (see illustration 2).

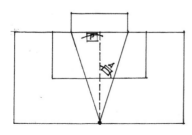

Illustration 2: If there is a defending teammate (A) standing inside the shooting angle, the goalkeeper must position slightly to the left.

Somebody may think that, if the correct position of the goalkeeper is along the bisecting line (see diagram 1), the closer the keeper gets to the opponent in possession of the ball the smaller the space the opponent can use to shoot at goal (by contrast, if the goalkeeper were standing along the goal line, the shooting angle that the opponent has at his disposal would be the same as the size of the goal - 8 yards - minus the space the goal-keeper is occupying). In this case, it would be easy for the goalkeeper to save the opponent's shot and prevent a goal from being scored: it would be enough for him to run to the ball as quickly as possible! However, if he fails to intercept the ball he will likely be beaten by a chip over his head.

In the case of a diving save, the goalkeeper must also consider the sides of the triangle; in fact, in this type of saving technique the ball must be intercepted sideways and forwards, in the position nearest to the keep-er; in the case of a diving save, the two perpendicular lines are the spots that are nearest to the sides of the triangles (see illustration 3).

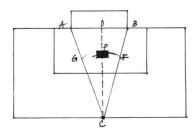

Illustration 3: If you draw the perpendicular lines of the triangle you can find the nearest points between the DC bisecting line and the sides of the triangle AC and BC. As you can see, the PF and PG lines are not parallel to the goal line.

Considering what we have said up to now, it is evident that the judgements and technical tasks that help the goalkeeper to find and take up the best positions are highly complex; therefore, there is not a unique model for positioning. It is necessary to consider all the physical and athletic attributes of each single player in addition to all the basic principles we have explained above.

In order to make things easier and clearer, we can consider some basic positioning principles:

1. The farther the ball is off the penalty box, the farther the goal keeper must move off the goal in order to get greater control over the whole area;
2. If the ball is inside the penalty box, it would be advisable for the goalkeeper to position inside the goal area.

However, in the case of an advanced position as explained in point no.1, the goalkeeper must take into proper account both the position of the ball and the possibility the opponent has to shoot at goal. For example, if the ball is at midfield or in the opposition's half of the field, the correct position for the goalkeeper is outside his penalty box, as if he were an "assistant sweeper" who is ready to save possible long balls or back passes made by his own teammates.

By contrast, if the ball is about 20 yards off the goal line, in a central position and the opponent is likely to shoot at goal, the best position for the goalkeeper is close to the edge of his six-yard area.

In the second case, if the ball is positioned on the flank, at a distance of about 10 to 12 yards from the goal line, it is advisable for the goal-keeper to stand along the bisecting line, at a distance that allows him to save the ball at the opponent's feet in case the attacker loses control of the ball. On the other hand, if the opponent manages to keep possession of the ball, the goalkeeper must stand in the correct "posture", waiting for the attacker to shoot. In fact, in this situation it is important to reduce the goal mouth to the shooter; nevertheless, this action should never compromise the goalkeeper's performance and reduce his reaction time. In short, if the keeper reduces the space between the ball and himself - from 12 to 3 yards, for example - he covers the opponent's shooting angle, but at the same time reduces the distance the ball needs to travel to beat him, thus decreasing the time he has at his disposal to save the ball (see illus. 4).

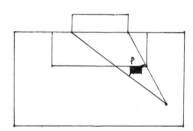

Illustration 4: The goalkeeper restricts the opponent's shooting angle, but also reduces the distance the ball needs to travel to beat him.

A skillful goalkeeper is able to predict the opponent's movements in order to anticipate him and choose the best position to make a save. When it is not possible to save the ball directly at the opponent's feet, the best waiting position is at a distance of about 6 to 7 yards from the ball.

Another important quality for a good goalkeeper is the ability to synchronize his movements with the action of the attacking opponent who is shooting at goal. In simpler words, the keeper must adjust the time he takes to prepare to make a save to the moves his opponent makes before kicking the ball. When the attacker is standing at a distance of about 18 to 20 yards and is swinging his kicking leg backwards, the goalkeeper must jump forward quickly (eccentric phase) and prepare to get enough power to push into the dive (concentric phase).

If the little pre-jump forward is performed in synch with the opponent's movement, it will help the goalkeeper to both get the elastic energy (eccentric phase) that he will need in the following pushing phase (concentric phase) and also reduce the distance between the ball and himself.

By contrast, if the opponent in possession of the ball is standing at a close distance (10 to 12 yards), the goalkeeper does not have enough time to make the pre-jump forward; in this case, the "loading" phase (eccentric phase) and the following push (concentric phase) will occur without making any movement forward, but directly on the spot.

We conclude by saying that a good goalkeeper must be able to use several pieces of information to choose the right time to begin a movement and the best moment to introduce another one. He must perfectly handle isolated or collective actions occurring simultaneously and also synchronize his movements to those of his opponent, which is still more important.

When the attacking maneuver built by the opposing team develops on the flanks of the field, the goalkeeper should move backward and position closer to the far post, rather than move forward towards the near post (see illustration 5); in fact, this position will help the goalkeeper leave the line and make a high save in the air and will also help him control the movements of both his teammates and his opponents inside the penalty area.

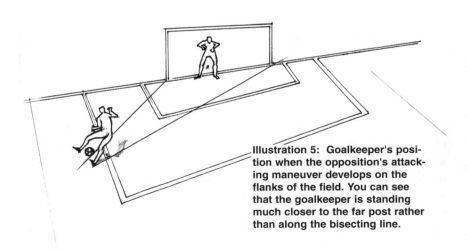

Illustration 5: Goalkeeper's position when the opposition's attacking maneuver develops on the flanks of the field. You can see that the goalkeeper is standing much closer to the far post rather than along the bisecting line.

When the player in possession of the ball is standing inside the penalty box near the goal line at an angle that will not allow him to take a direct shot on goal, the goalkeeper must move opposite his opponent and position at a distance of about two feet in front of the near post. This slightly advanced position will prevent the keeper from deflecting the ball into the net if he dives either to the right or to the left to catch the ball (see diagram 6a). However, he should avoid moving too much off the near post (two or three yards, for example): in fact, if the opponent in possession of the ball makes a back-pass directly in front of the goal instead of shooting, the player receiving the pass could easily shoot and score because the whole goal mouth would be totally unguarded and the goalkeeper would not have enough time to recover and take up the best position to try to make the save, since he is too far off the goal mouth (see diagram 6b).

Illustration 6a: In this case the best position the goalkeeper can take is slightly in front of the near post; in this situation, if he deflects the ball sideways, the ball will run over the goal line.

Illustration 6b:The goalkeeper has moved too much off the near post; if the opposing attacker passes the ball backward to one of his teammates, the keeper is not able to cover the goal mouth.

1.1   The goalkeeper's movements

In order to take up the correct position, the goalkeeper must be able to move to the right, to the left or forward in relation to the movements of the ball. Nevertheless, while stepping to move sideways the goalkeeper must also consider all the possibilities his attacking opponent has to shoot at goal.

If the ball carrier can easily shoot, the goalkeeper must move quickly, taking short and quick steps sideways, always ready to take the best "posture" to make a save.

On the other hand, if the opponent can is not in a position take a direct shot on goal and makes a cross-field pass - from right to left, for example - to one of his teammates, the goalkeeper cannot step sideways, but must move very rapidly, "crossing" the first step; in fact, the goalkeeper's main purpose in this situation is not to take the right "posture", but to take up the best position in relation to the ball in the shortest time possible.

1.2   DRILLS
To improve positioning technique

Drill n.1

Purpose:
Get control over the penalty area and the six yard box.

Procedure:
The goalkeeper moves sideways, taking short and quick steps from one post to the other, horizontal to the goal line.

Variation:
The goalkeeper moves sideways from one post to the other, drawing a semicircle.

Number of repetitions:
About ten before suitable recovery.

Notes:
The goalkeeper memorizes the reference points between his position and the goal area, the penalty box, the semicircle, the penalty spot and the opposite goal.

Especially suggested for:
All goalkeepers during the very first days of pre-season training camp;
Youth keepers during the standard week.

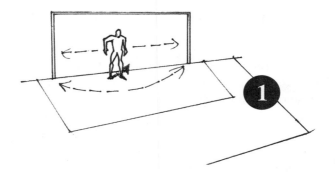

Drill n.2

Purpose:
Get control over the goal area and the six yard box.

Procedure:
After mastering drill #1, the goalkeeper is blindfolded and must move inside the goal from one post to the other along the goal line, trying not to lose his bearings. Randomly, the coach calls "shot!" and throws throws the ball at the keeper's stomach and the keeper catches it and brings it up to his chest.

Variation:
The keeper moves from one post to the other drawing a semicircle in front of the goal.

Number of repetitions:
5-6 per set with a suitable recovery between sets.

Notes:
The keeper must learn to orientate without any points of reference (posts, penalty spot...).

Especially suggested for:
All goalkeepers during the very first days of pre-season training camp;
Youth keepers when reviewing positioning practice every month.

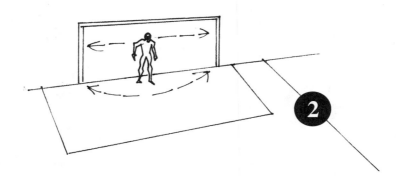

Purpose:

Get control over the penalty area and the six yard box. Master the sense of positioning.

Procedure:

The goalkeeper is completely blindfolded and is standing in the middle of the goal; he must move to take up the correct position: his sole reference is the sound of the ball the coach is bouncing on the ground. If the keeper finds it difficult to take the right position, the coach continues to bounce the ball until the player positions correctly. When he takes up the best position, the coach throws the ball at his stomach and the goalkeeper immediately catches it with his hands and brings it up to his chest to protect it.

Variation n.1:

The coach uses his voice instead of bouncing the ball on the ground.

Variation n.2:

The coach uses both the bouncing ball and the sound of his voice.

Number of repetitions:

5-6 per set with suitable recovery.

Notes:

With this exercise the goalkeeper must learn how to take up the best position using only his hearing.

Especially suggested for:

All goalkeepers early on in the pre-season training camp;

Youth keepers when reviewing positioning practice every month.

Drill n.4

Purpose:
Developing positioning skills.

Procedure:
Starting from the goal line, the goalkeeper places a flat cone on the field to show the bisecting line and the best position to catch the ball in relation to the position of the ball that is lying between the coach's feet.

Number of repetitions:
Up to 10 with before suitable recovery.

Notes:
In this exercise the goalkeeper talks to the coach and consequently learns to find the right bisecting line and take the best position compared to the position of the ball.

Especially suggested for:
All goalkeepers early on in the pre-season training camp;
Youth keepers when reviewing positioning practice every month.

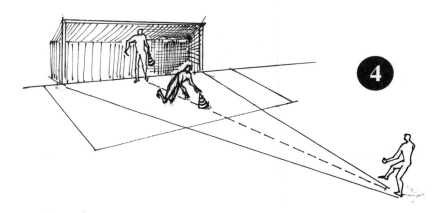

Drill n.5

Purpose:
Developing positioning skills and finding the best posture to catch the ball.

Procedure:
Starting from the goal line, the goalkeeper moves to take up the best position along the bisecting line of the triangle and waits for the coach to shoot the ball. The ball is kicked only if the goalkeeper is standing in the correct position.

Variation:
The coach is standing at a distance of 3 yds from the ball; when he gives the signal, the keeper takes the best position to try to save the shot.

Number of repetitions:
5-6 per set; good recovery between

sets; no more than 2 sets per session.

Notes:

There is a slight difference between the two exercises, because in the first situation the goalkeeper has all the time he needs to find the right position, while in the second he is forced to move rapidly to save the coach's quick shot. It is clear that in the second situation the keeper may find himself in an unstable posture, with his weight forward or backward and his legs out of position. This exercise is very similar to what happens in a game and illustrates that taking up the right posture and catching position is fundamental to successful shot stopping.

Especially suggested for:

All goalkeepers when reviewing positioning technique every month.

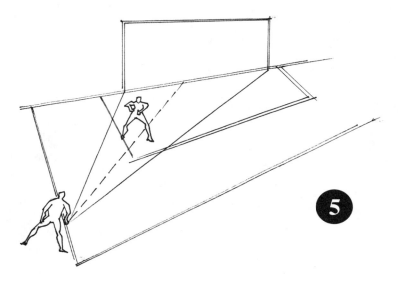

Drill n.6

Purpose:

Develop positioning skills and take the best posture to catch the ball.

Procedure:

Two coaches are standing in a central position about 16-18 yards off the goal and pass the ball to each other. At first, the keeper must follow the movements of the ball and position accordingly; when he sees one of the two coaches stop the ball to take a shot on goal, he adjusts his position and takes the correct posture to make the save.

Variation:

The same exercise can be performed with the two coaches standing to either side of the goal mouth rather than in a central position

Number of repetitions:

3-4 repetitions per set; suitable recovery between sets; no more than 2 sets per session.

Notes:

Through these exercises you can train the goalkeeper to find the correct position while moving and in situations of dynamic balance; moreover, they will accustom him to timing his leg push and movements in synchrony with the shooter's movements.

Especially suggested for:

All goalkeepers when reviewing positioning technique every month.

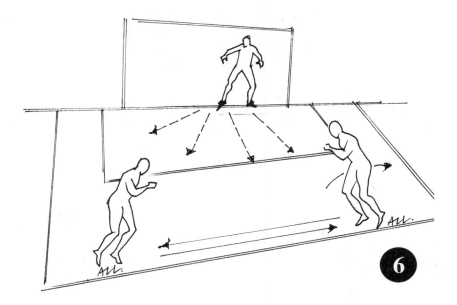

Drill n.7

Purpose:

Improve positioning skills and catching posture while moving at speed.

Procedure:

Three goalkeepers or more (n.1, n.2, n.3) dribble the ball inside a 6-yard wide square area marked in one corner of the penalty box. When the coach gives the signal (calls "Number 2!" for example), that keeper must sprint to take the best position and save the shot.

Number of repetitions:

No more than 4-5 shots per keeper; no more than 2 sets per session.

Notes:

In addition to helping improve his sense of positioning in dynamic situations, this exercise also teaches the keeper the correct movements to make when he is standing far from the posts or when he is positioned inside the goal: short and quick steps (like in a sprint) when he has to get to the goal; short and quick steps sideways when he has to follow the path of the shot.

Especially suggested for:

All goalkeepers when revising positioning skills every month;

Youth keepers when reviewing positioning technique every month.

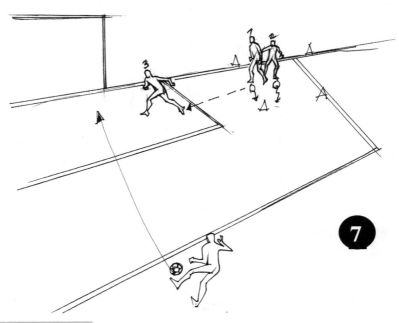

Drill n.8

Purpose:

Improve positioning technique and catching posture while moving at speed.

Procedure:

The goalkeeper moves rapidly inside three goals (n.1, n.2 and n.3) 6 yds wide and positioned 5-6 yds from each other; the keeper always starts from the central goal (n.2) and when the coach gives the signal ("Goal Number 3!" for example), the goalkeeper must sprint to posi-

tion inside that goal and save the coach's shot. The position of the balls should vary from about 12-16 yds.

Number of repetitions:

No more than 3-4 per set; suitable recovery between sets; no more than 2 sets per session.

Notes:

In addition to helping improve his sense of positioning in dynamic situations, this exercise also teaches the keeper the correct movements to make both when he is standing far from the posts and when he is positioned inside the goal: short and quick steps (like in a sprint) when he has to get tot he goal; short and quick steps sideways when he has to follow the path of the shot.

Especially suggested for:
All goalkeepers when refreshing positioning technique every month; youth keepers when practicing positioning skills every month.

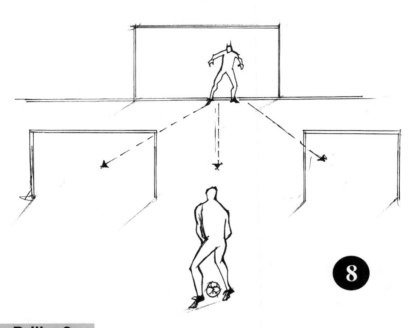

Drill n.9

Purpose:
Improve positioning technique and catching posture while moving at speed.

Procedure:
The coach is standing inside the 6-yd box and simulates a cross coming from the flank; the keeper must deflect the ball in the air to make it turn off the goal and fall inside the penalty area; an assistant coach or player will take a first -time shot

and the keeper must take up a new position to try to make the save.

Number of repetitions:
No more than 4-5 shots per keeper; no more than 2 sets per session; suitable recovery between sets.

Notes:
In addition to helping improve positioning technique in dynamic situations, this exercise also allows the keeper to practice moving correctly and deflecting the ball in the

air, as well as his capacity to decide whether it is advisable to come out and make a low save immediately after the attacking opponent controls the ball, or wait for the shot.

All goalkeepers in training sessions focusing on game situations.

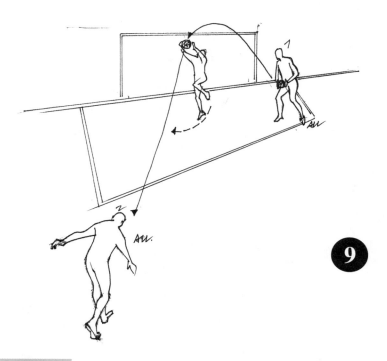

Drill n.10

Purpose:
Improve positioning technique, catching posture and decision making while moving at speed.

Procedure:
The coach places 4 balls (numbered 1-4) inside the penalty area; another ball is shot at goal directly to have the goalkeeper make a catch (a diving save is also allowed); immediately afterwards, the coach calls the number of the ball (1-4) that he is going to kick; after trying to save the first shot, the keeper must read the new shooting situation rapidly and decide whether it is better to come off the line and make a low save at the coach's feet or wait for the shot in an upright position.

Number of repetitions:
No more than 4-5 shots per keeper; no more than 2 sets per session; suitable recovery between sets.

Notes:

In addition to helping improve the sense of positioning in dynamic situations, this exercise also allows the keeper to practice moving correctly, catching technique and the capacity to decide quickly whether it is advisable to come out and make a low save after the attacker controls the ball or wait for the shot.

Especially suggested for:

All goalkeepers in training sessions focusing on game situations.

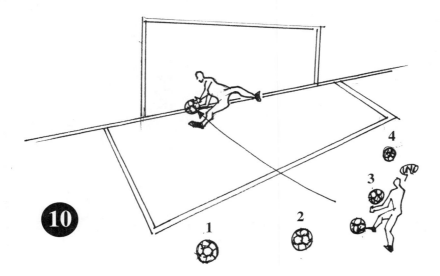

The goalkeeper is the first line of attack in a soccer team: among the various duties the goalkeeper has to perform, not only does he have to prevent goals from being scored, he also has to restart the attacking maneuver by either kicking the ball with his feet or throwing it with his hands. How many times has a goalkeeper's successful kick or throw resulted in a clear opportunity for his team to score a goal? On the other hand, how many times has he made a wrong decision that has prevented a successful offensive build-up, or even worse, that has allowed the opposition to win possession of the ball and become dangerous themselves on attack? A recent study carried out on the performances of the best goalkeepers in the world showed that the attacking actions (kicks, throws and goal-kicks) account for 64% of all the functions that keepers generally fulfill. If you analyze this data carefully, you can easily understand that it is necessary to "enrich" your training sessions with special exercises that help focus greater attention on distribution technique. The keeper can deliver the ball using either his hands or his feet; both throwing and kicking the ball can produce favorable and unfavorable situations.

2.1 Kicking the ball

Goalkeepers are responsible for taking goal-kicks so that the opposing players are not standing near the penalty box; in this way, greater distance is kept between the defensive line and the goal. The kicking technique involves the goalkeeper taking a short run up at an angle to the kicking direction, placing the plant foot beside the ball and swinging the kicking foot forward to strike the ball powerfully. While keeping an eye on the ball, the keeper bends slightly backward, stretches out his leg and kicks the ball with the inside of the foot making contact with the lower part of the ball.

When the goalkeeper intercepts the opposition's attacking maneuver and realizes that he can start a sudden counterattack, he generally makes a long kick so that his attacking teammates can exploit large cleared spaces upfield. Keepers also take long kicks to release the ball when they want to make their team move upward into the opposition's half of the field; this is a common tactical strategy especially used when a team wants to break pressure and counterpress the opposition.

There are two ways for the goalkeeper to kick the ball over long distances: a punt with the instep and a drop kick.

The difference between these techniques is the trajectory of the ball after being kicked. A drop kick gives a flatter path to the ball, which is more useful in starting the counterattack and is much easier for the attacking teammates to control. On the other hand, punts are generally easier to perform: this is the reason why most goalkeepers all over the world usually prefer this technique to deliver the ball.

In order to punt the ball the keeper takes a short run up and kicks the ball with the instep. He drops the ball down to the ground using the hand opposite to the kicking foot (if he kicks the ball with the right foot, he will drop it down with his left hand and vice versa) so that he can drive the leg with greater energy and consequently take a more powerful kick. The foot will make contact with the ball as close as possible to the ground so as to avoid excessively high trajectories.

By contrast, when the goalkeeper drop kicks the ball, his foot makes contact with the ball immediately after it bounces on the ground. In order to take a perfectly timed drop kick, the keeper must stand directly behind the ball and let it drop down to the ground with both hands. This technique is very useful in windy conditions because the low path of the ball makes it better for driving into the wind. Moreover, it is also advisable to avoid using this technique in case of slow pitches and uneven grounds.

It is advisable that goalkeepers practice both kicking techniques in training sessions so that they are able to choose the best solution depending on circumstances in official matches. Often, a successful kick is the will lead directly to a shooting action.

Goal-kicks are also up to modern goalkeepers since it is no longer acceptable that their field teammates put the ball back into play in those situations. In fact, if the goalkeeper takes the goal kick, he allows his team to move upward towards the midfield line, so that they can defend far from their own goal, if necessary, and start their attack closer to the opposition's goal.

2.2 Throwing the ball

Most teams in modern soccer try to avoid making long passes at random since they generally tend to build "the plot of the game" starting from their back lines, so that it becomes much easier for them to arrange the offensive build-up. Throwing the ball with one's hands is the most suitable way for starting the team's attacking action. Even though throws are usually much shorter than kicks, throwing the ball allows the team to start the offensive build-up in a much more rapid and accurate manner; furthermore, it is easier for field players to receive and control the ball.

When the player receiving the pass is standing just outside the penalty box, it is advisable for the goalkeeper to roll the ball on the ground like in bowling. In order to perform this throw successfully, the goalkeeper places his left leg in front of the other one to avoid knocking against the knee on the same side of the throwing hand (the right one, in this case) and points it towards the receiving teammate; he swings the throwing arm forward and lets the ball roll on the ground, always trying to keep it low (see illustration 1) - the transition of the ball from the hand to the ground should be very smooth. On the other hand, when the goalkeeper's teammate is standing unguarded at a distance of about 20 to 25 yards, it is advisable to make a javelin throw where the ball starts in the palm of the hand beside the head and is thrown straight forward as the keeper steps into the throw (see illustration 2).

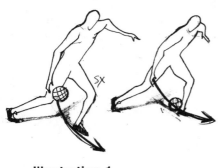

Illustration 1

Illustration 2

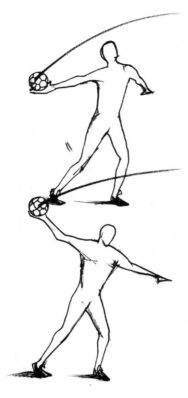

The sidearm throw is the most suitable technique to throw the ball over longer distances. In this case, the ball is held sideways slightly behind the hip, the left hand points forward as if it were showing the direction, the right hand with the palm turned upward holds the ball and throws it with the arm perfectly stretched outward and upward at the same time (see illustration 3). If it is performed correctly, this distribution technique can travel as far as a goal-kick and is useful to start the offensive build-up quickly and accurately.

There is another technique that goalkeepers can use to throw the ball with their hands which is very similar to the discus throw technique; it is used to deliver the ball over long distances, but the spin given to the ball can make it difficult to control.

One of the main principles underlying any type of throwing technique is that the ball should be delivered in the direction opposite to where it first came from. It is fundamental that the goalkeeper's field teammates also know this principle, since they must move wide to elude the marking and receive - undisturbed - the ball thrown by their keeper.

Illustration 3

2.3 DRILLS
To improve distribution technique

Drill n.1

Purpose:
Develop kicking technique.

Procedure:
The goalkeeper places the ball at the edge of the 6-yd box and tries to kick the ball into one of the two square areas (12x12 yds) marked at the far right and far left near the midfield line.

Number of repetitions:
6-8 goal-kicks after suitable warm up.

Notes:
In this exercise the goalkeeper learns to kick the ball accurately. It is advisable to have the keeper kick the ball with both the right and left foot.

Especially suggested for:
All goalkeepers in training sessions focusing on distribution technique. Remember to reduce the distance between the two squares and the goal when coaching young keepers.

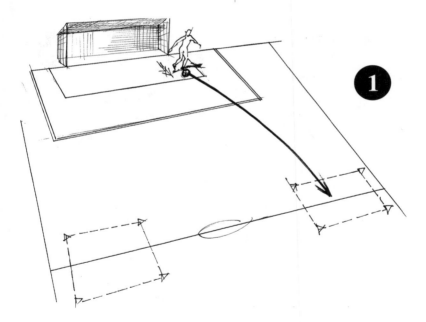

Purpose:

Develop kicking technique.

Procedure:

After making a high save in the air, the goalkeeper kicks the ball back from inside the 6-ye box with a punt or a drop-kick aimed at one of the three square areas about 20 yds wide (n.1, n.2 and n.3) marked in the opposing half of the field. The keeper should be advised to take a drop-kick when the ball has to be delivered into the central square; in this case, the ball will describe a flatter and quicker path and it will be easier for the attacking player to develop a successful shooting action.

Number of repetitions:

6-8 after suitable warm up.

Notes:

In this exercise the goalkeeper learns to kick the ball accurately. It is advisable to have the keeper kick the ball with both the right and left foot.

Especially suggested for:

All goalkeepers in training sessions focusing on kicking technique.

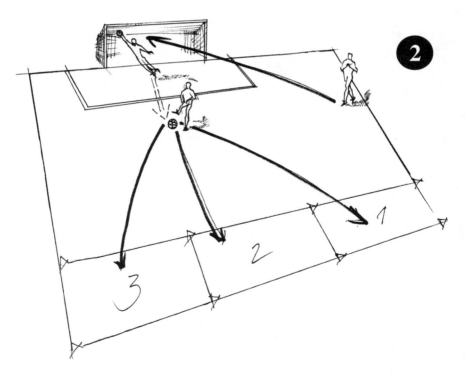

Purpose:

Develop distribution technique both throwing and kicking the ball.

Procedure:

After making a high save in the air or a diving save, the goalkeeper kicks the ball back from inside the 6-ye box with a punt or a drop-kick aimed at one of the two goals about 10-12 yds wide marked with agility poles placed near the touch lines about 40-50 yds from the goal. The two goals are designated "Even Goal" and "Uneven Goal". After shooting, the coach shouts a number. If it is an even number, the goalkeeper must kick the ball towards the "Even Goal", and if it is an uneven number he must aim for the "Uneven Goal".

Variation n.1:

The goalkeeper delivers the ball by kicking and throwing alternately.

Variation n.1:

The goalkeeper can put the ball back in play not only after a save, but also after a back pass; in this case, he is only allowed to kick the ball with his feet.

Number of repetitions:

6-8 after suitable warm up.

Notes:

In this exercise the goalkeeper learns to kick the ball accurately.

Especially suggested for:

All goalkeepers in training sessions focusing on distribution technique. Remember to reduce the distance between the goals and the penalty box when coaching youth keepers.

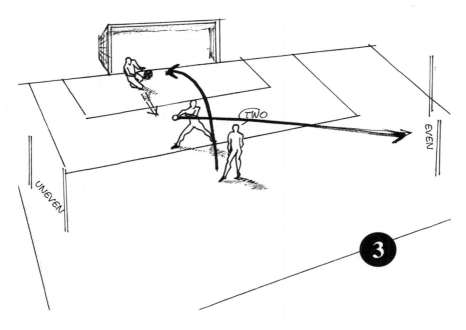

Purpose:

Develop distribution technique both throwing and kicking the ball.

Procedure:

After catching a shot (either a high save in the air or a diving save), the goalkeeper kicks the ball back to one of the two teammates standing near the touch line more or less at midfield. One of the two field players will turn his back to the keeper, simulating an unfavorable situation (for example, an opponent putting pressure on him) that indicates he cannot receive the ball. This means that the keeper must look at the positions of the two players quickly before delivering the ball. If both teammates turn their backs to him, the keeper must take a drop-kick or a punt as far as possible towards the center of the pitch.

Variation:

The goalkeeper delivers the ball by kicking and throwing alternately.

Number of repetitions:

6-8 after suitable warm up.

Notes:

Performing this exercise the goalkeeper learns to deliver the ball accurately both kicking it and throwing it and also improves his capacity to read the situation at a tactical level.

Especially suggested for:

All goalkeepers in training sessions focusing on distribution technique. Remember to reduce the distance between the goalkeeper and the field players when coaching youth keepers.

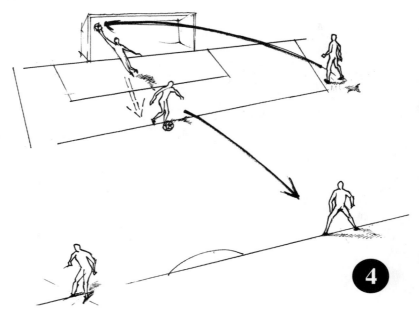

Drill n.5

Purpose:
Acquire and develop kicking technique.

Procedure:
The coach gives a back pass to the goalkeeper who has to control it with one touch and kick it back towards on of the three goals placed on the field as follows: one in the center near the midfield line (goal n.2), one on the left (goal n.1) and one on the right (goal n.3) near the touchlines about 20 yards from the goal line. When the coach passes the ball back to the keeper, he also tells him at what goal he must aim the ball.

Number of repetitions:
6-8 after suitable warm up.

Notes:
Performing this exercise the goalkeeper learns to kick the ball accurately; remember that in order to get to the central goal, the ball must have a high trajectory and if it is kicked towards one of the side goals it must follow a straight ground path.

Especially suggested for:
All goalkeepers in training sessions focusing on distribution technique. Remember to reduce the distance between the goals and the penalty area when coaching youth keepers.

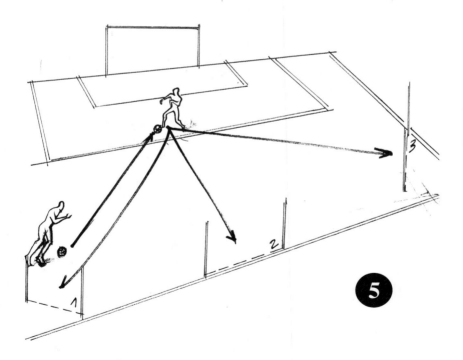

Drill n.6

Purpose:
Acquire and develop kicking technique.

Procedure:
After intercepting the ball with a high catch in the air or a diving save, the goalkeeper follows the signals the coach gives him and reacts accordingly: right arm up means that the keeper must take a punt or a drop kick towards the left area of the field; left arm up means the ball has to be kicked towards the right side; both arms up means that the keeper must kick the ball centrally upfield.

Variation:
The keeper can also put the ball back into play by throwing it.

Number of repetitions:
6-8 after suitable warm up.

Notes:
Performing this exercise the goalkeeper learns to kick and throw the ball accurately while performing some basic tactical duties in relation to the signals the coach gives by moving his arms. This exercise simulates a situation that is very similar to real game situations.

Especially suggested for:
All goalkeepers in training sessions focusing on distribution technique.

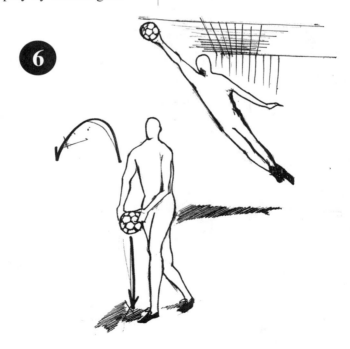

Drill n.7

Purpose:

Develop distribution technique both kicking and throwing the ball.

Procedure:

After catching the ball with a diving save, the goalkeeper releases it on the ground to one of his teammates standing laterally just outside the penalty box; this player simulates being pressed by the opposition and gives a back pass to the keeper. At this point, the coach moves to commit and disturb the keeper to force him to kick the ball quickly. The keeper must kick the ball towards one of his teammates accurately and without unnecessary touches.

Number of repetitions:

3-4 after suitable warm up.

Notes:

Performing this exercise the goalkeeper learns to kick the ball accurately in a situation of play that is very close to the real game. Wasting time or misreading the situation may result in the opposition intercepting the ball and shooting at goal.

Especially suggested for:

All goalkeepers in training sessions focusing on distribution technique.

Drill n.8

Purpose:
Acquire and develop kicking technique.

Procedure:
The coach gives a back pass to the goalkeeper who receives the pass, controls the ball with one touch and starts the offensive build-up by kicking the ball at one of the two small goals placed near the touch lines at a distance of about 18-20 yds from the goal line. The two goals (8-10 yds wide) are designated "Even Goal" and "Uneven Goal" respectively. When the coach passes the ball back to the keeper, he also calls a number. The keeper must make an accurate ground pass to the corresponding goal.

Number of repetitions:
7-8 kicks per goalkeeper.

Notes:
Performing this exercise the goalkeeper learns to kick the ball accurately in a situation of play that is very close to the real game. The coach must set how many touches of the ball the goalkeeper is allowed to control the ball (never more than three).

Especially suggested for:
All goalkeepers in training sessions focusing on kicking technique.

28

Drill n.9

Purpose:

Acquire and develop kicking technique.

Procedure:

The goalkeeper makes a ground pass to the coach standing in front of him at a distance of about 8-10 yds. The coach passes the ball back to the keeper, who has to give a first touch pass with a high and accurate trajectory to another goalkeeper standing in front of him at a distance of about 30-40 yds. This keeper also performs the same exercise, passing the ball to another teammate.

Number of repetitions:

7-8 kicks per goalkeeper.

Notes:

Performing this exercise the goalkeeper learns to kick the ball accurately in a situation of play that is very close to the real game. The coach must set how many touches of the ball the goalkeeper is allowed to control the ball (never more than three).

Especially suggested for:

All goalkeepers in training sessions focusing on kicking technique.

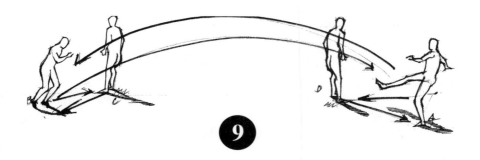

Being able to come out of the goal to save a ball is one of the basic technical requisites characterizing modern goalkeepers. In fact, attacking maneuvers in modern soccer are increasingly developing on the flanks of the pitch, with the ball being crossed inward towards the penalty box, both because it is increasingly difficult to break through centrally and because of the tactical systems that many coaches of the new generation choose for their teams. This tactical solution also emerges from the statistical survey on the last World Cup, which confirms that most attacking actions originate from the flanks of the field. In these cases, it is very important for a team to play a goalkeeper that is able to come out of the goal to make a save, also because the defender is in a slightly unfavorable position compared to his attacking opponent since he has to focus his attention on both the ball and the movements of the opponent he is marking.

A good goalkeeper with a modern mentality should play an "active" role in checking the development of the opposition's offensive build-up; in this way, he will no longer act as the most withdrawn defender exclusively, who simply waits and hopes to catch the opponent's shot on goal, but he will play as an "active player" who tries to break the opposition's offensive actions before they can shoot at goal.

Consequently, a new way of conceiving the figure and role of the goalkeeper is developing: the keeper is no longer a "spectator" in front of the opposition's attacking play, but he becomes an "absolute" protagonist of events. In practice, according to the old conception of the goalkeeper's role, the decision to handle a crossed ball with a high catch in the air or a ground save was generally taken only when the opponent in possession of the ball was making the cross; this meant that the goalkeeper came out of the goal to save the cross only and exclusively if there was enough time and space to do it - for example, in case of slow crosses, balls describing very high trajectories, if the opponent made a poor cross in the wrong direction, if there were relatively few players inside the box, etc. By contrast, according to the modern idea of the goalkeeper's position, the keeper can decide to come out and save a high ball even before the opponent makes the cross. This requires the goalkeeper to develop a completely different mental approach and also a new tactical predisposition of his

31

role, beginning from the standard starting position; in fact, the goalkeeper is no longer standing "rooted" down on the goal line, but starts from a more advanced position (see illustration 1).

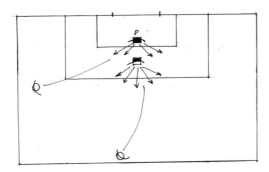

Diagram 1: This diagram shows the position of the goalkeeper in relation to the position of the ball: the farther the ball is from the penalty area, the more the goalkeeper has to come out of the goal line to have a better "coverage" of the whole box.

The goalkeeper can come out of the goal and save the ball in different ways, but the most used techniques include:
- high saves in the air, with or without diving;
- low saves on the ground, with or without diving;
- punching save - with 1 or 2 punches - with or without diving.

3.1 High saves

Being able to come out of the goal for balls high in the air is a basic skill of critical importance for good goalkeepers; this technical movement, in fact, is also useful for all the defensive line. A goalkeeper jumping high to make a clean catch of the ball in the air in the middle of his box breaks the opposition's attacking action, preventing his defending teammates from having to sweep the ball away (which may also prove dangerous), or the opposition from shooting at goal.

Preparing to come out and make a save
The waiting position the goalkeeper takes before making a high save is generally defined as"high" position since the pushing angles of the lower limbs are wide open (see diagram 3); this waiting stance provides less leg strength (which is not important in this situation), but more agility and quickness in the movements the keeper makes to step sideways and forward (this is a fundamental requisite to get to the ball at the right time) (see illustration 2).

Illustration 2: The posture preparing for a high save is commonly defined "high" position since the angles of the lower limb joints are very wide open and cannot provide much strength, but allow to make rapid and quick movements sideways and forward to get to the ball.

This ready position is common to any technique used to make aerial saves; moreover, the goalkeeper should also get accustomed to warning his teammates of his coming out by shouting something like "mine!" or "keeper!".

On the other hand, the leg position changes depending on the direction from which the cross comes.

If the ball is crossed with a high trajectory centrally, from a distance of about 35 to 40 yards, the goalkeeper starts from a very advanced position in front of the goal and cannot keep his feet close and parallel to each other, but he instead staggers his feet slightly one just behind the other so as to generate extra boost forward to move towards the ball. (see illustration 3)

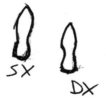

Illustration 3: This position of the feet helps provide extra boost when sprinting forward to get to the ball.

By contrast, if the high ball is crossed from the flanks of the field, as happens in most cases, the goalkeeper must keep his legs slightly wide apart, forming a sort of "L", with the foot nearest to the direction of the ball almost parallel to the goal line and the other foot almost square to that line (see illustration 4).

Illustration 4: Correct feet position to prepare to save crosses coming from the right flank.

A cross coming from the flanks of the field can land at four different points inside the penalty box, as shown in the diagram no.5 below:
- around the near post;
- at the edge of the goal area around the near corner;
- in the area between the edge of the goal box and the penalty spot;
- at the far corner of the goal box

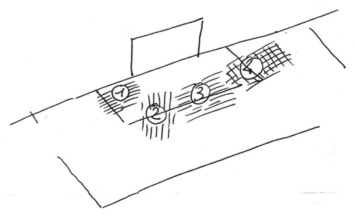

Diagram 5: Landing zones of a ball crossed from the left flank of the field:
1. the near post (zone no.1)
2. the near corner of the goal box (zone 2)
3. the area between the edge of the six-yard box and the penalty spot (zone 3)
4. the far corner of the goal area, opposite to where the ball comes from (zone 4).

If the ball lands in zone no.1 (around the near post), the goalkeeper starts his movement moving the right foot (which is the farthest from the ball) towards the ball and positions so as to stand square to the cross; afterwards, he takes a quick run up: the last step going into the jump must be longer than the others for additional boost; the other leg is raised with the knee bent to provide protection in case of collisions with an opponent. The arms are raised upward and the hands get to the ball first to catch it at the highest point possible, above the players' heads so as to prevent the opposition from rushing in and heading the ball away before it gets to the keeper's hands. Moreover, the goalkeeper must also get used to catching the ball with both hands with his arms extended, and then bend his elbows to bring the ball to his chest in a protected position after the catch.

The goalkeeper should land on both feet, preferably, in order to avoid losing his balance or getting injured when landing on the ground (ankle or knee sprains are likely to occur with one foot landings). This catching and landing technique is common to all high saves.

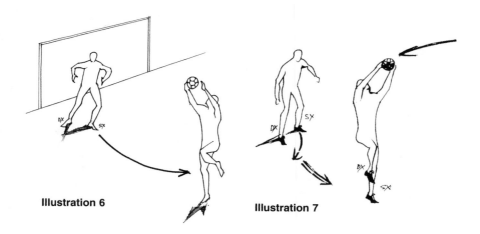

Illustration 6

Illustration 7

If the ball lands in zone 2 (at the near corner of the six-yard box), the goalkeeper moves his feet in the same way described above for balls landing in sector no.1 and positions square to the ball direction (see illustration 6).

If the ball lands in zone 3 (that is in the area between the goal box and the penalty spot), first of all the goalkeeper moves his left foot (the foot nearest to the flank of the field where the cross comes from) so as to position his body square to where the ball will land (the penalty spot, for example) and take as many steps as needed to achieve maximum power to drive towards the ball. The last push step into the jump is very important since it must help trunk rotation while in the air (leftward, in this case) to intercept the path of the ball (see illustration 7). It is clear that the pushing leg is the one nearest to the flank of the field where the cross comes from, while the other leg is bent at the knee to protect the goalkeeper in case he crashes into an opponent while catching the ball.

If the ball lands in zone 4 (the opposite corner of the six-yard box), the goalkeeper takes a quick crossover step with the leg nearest to the flank of the field where the ball comes from passing across the other leg which acts as a pivot for the body to turn towards the supposed landing spot, while the eyes are constantly kept on the ball (see illustration 8). In this way, the goalkeeper's body is turned towards the place where the ball is going to land (zone 4), while his eyes are fixed on the ball. Before making the final jump (which must be performed with the same leg used to take the crossover step), the keeper takes quick steps into the run up to generate greater power that will allow him to make a better "take-off" to achieve proper rotation and height of the body towards the ball (see illustration 9).

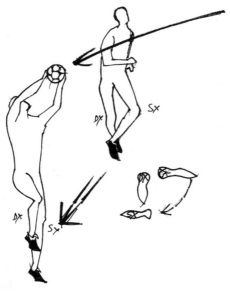

Illustration 8: This illustration shows all the steps that allow the goalkeeper to take a crossover step. The left leg passes across the right one.

36

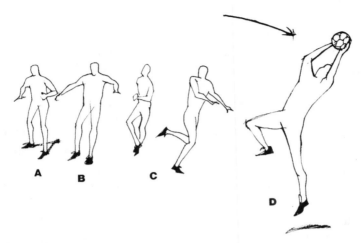

Illustration 9: This illustration shows the sequence of movements the goalkeeper makes to "catch" a cross coming from his right and landing in zone no.4, supposedly.
A: crossover step always keeping the eyes fixed on the ball;
B: run up steps with the body facing the spot where the ball is supposed to land, but always keeping the eyes fixed on the ball;
C: run up steps and take-off with the right leg helping body rotation and with the left leg bent at the knee for protection;
D: the goalkeeper intercepts the cross in the air with the body totally facing the ball.

If the ball is difficult and/or risky to catch (due to heavy traffic in the area or because the ball is wet and slimy), it is advisable for the goalkeeper to punch the ball away. The keeper can use a one- or two-handed punch.

Two-handed punch: if the ball is crossed from in front, it is advisable for the goalkeeper to take a short run up, shout "mine!" in a firm tone and clear the ball away using a two handed punch so as to have the largest surface possible making contact with the ball and generate more power to drive the ball as far away as possible. In this case, the goalkeeper keeps his fists together with the thumbs behind the fists and strikes the ball with the flat surface between the knuckles and the finger joints after "exploding" the arms upward rapidly through the ball.

One-handed punch: this technique is used preferably when the ball is crossed from either flank of the field; in this case, a smaller surface of the hand makes contact with the ball, but there is better coordination in the movement. Moreover, it is also possible to generate much power to box the ball towards the flank of the field opposite to the direction of the ball.

3.2 Diving saves

There are some situations where the goalkeeper has no choice but to come out of the goal and intercept the ball in a reckless and spectacular manner. In these cases, in addition to the particular technical move, he also needs courage and valor. This technique is especially used to catch balls in mid-air or balls bouncing in an "unexpected" manner near the goalkeeper (for example, when the ball rebounds on a player unintentionally, in case of poor ball controls or strange tackles between players, and so on). In these cases, the goalkeeper should try to anticipate the attacking opponent and come out of the goal unexpectedly to make a spectacular and reckless save in order to surprise the opponent. The goalkeeper takes a short run up to dive forward, also without taking special care of the proper diving technique, trying to catch the ball or punch it away with both fists closed together. He will land on the ground on his hip and side if he manages to catch the ball, on his chest if he punches the ball away with his fists.

If you are coaching youth goalkeepers, it is advisable to train this particular technical move using suitable mats to cushion the impact with the ground.

3.3 Ground saves

Ground saving is a technical action that goalkeepers use rather frequently during the course of a match, especially if their team applies the offside tactical strategy and presses the opposition upward. However, there are some particular situations that go beyond the team tactical strategies where the goalkeeper is forced to make a ground save; these situations include:

1. when he has to handle a ball breaking through his defensive line and getting to an opponent standing in a favorable position to shoot at goal from a close distance or, in any case, inside the penalty box;
2. when he has to commit to an opponent who has dribbled the ball successfully past the last defender in a 1vs1 situation;
3. when he has to deal with crosses made from the goal line with the ball grazing the ground.

In addition to good saving technique, these situations also require of the goalkeeper much courage to put his hands - and also his head, on some occasions - where the opponents put their feet.

In this regard, particular attention should be focused on the "gift" of courage.

This quality should not be confused with irresponsibility, but should be considered as the capacity to dominate and control one's body in the most extreme situations; whatever technique the goalkeeper uses to save the ball, he can never "risk his arms" by his eyes, but should always be aware of what he is going to do and have enough self-control to take the right decision at the right time.

The exercises from diagram 3.g.10 to diagram 3.g.18 are a simple coaching progression that helps train and stimulate a sense of courage in goalkeepers.

Going back to the situations where the goalkeeper is required to make ground saves, in the case of a pass breaking through the defensive line (point no.1), if the keeper is able to read how the opposition's play is developing, he has to sprint towards the ball coming out of the goal to make a timely ground save and anticipate the opponent diving as close as possible to the ground. The arms are extended forward with the hands wide open, ready to catch the ball and protect the chest.

On the other hand, when the goalkeeper is late compared to the opposition's maneuver and realizes that he can no longer catch the ball, he can only defend the goal using all his body, standing in a diagonal position compared to the direction of the ball in order to induce the opponent to shoot at him; in this "desperate" situation it may happen that the keeper manages to touch the ball, is beaten by a ball chipped over his head or takes a penalty. In short, it is important to say that for a goalkeeper to perform this technical action successfully, he absolutely needs to be able to "read" the development of the opposition's play and be perfectly aware of his own reaction time.

When the attacking opponent manages to dribble past a defender inside the penalty box and arrives in front of the goalkeeper (point no.2), the keeper must be very firm and cool to avoid rushing at the opponent; he must wait for the "moves" the ball carrier makes and act accordingly. If the attacker keeps ball possession, there is a typical 1vs1 situation; in this case, the goalkeeper takes a "low" starting position keeping his legs slightly apart in order to move very rapidly in a small space; when the opponent is going to shoot at goal, he opens his legs wider apart so as to "find" the ground more easily in case he has to dive. At the beginning the goalkeeper waits for the opponent's movements and, as soon as the ball carrier makes a longer touch of the ball, he promptly sprints to make a ground save, or he stands until the opponent finally shoots, thus delaying the opponent's action and favoring a possible recovery move by one of his teammates. It is important for the keeper to always keep his eyes on the ball to avoid being deceived by the attacker's feints; moreover, he should also demonstrate that he can perfectly handle the situation covering the goal mouth, not losing his balance backward so as to induce the opponent to take hasty decisions. It is evident that reaction kick saves or saves made with any other part of the body are to be considered successful actions in those situations.

When an attacking opponent manages to get into the penalty box near the goal line after a combined maneuver or a dribble and can only choose the solution to play the ball backward towards an incoming teammate, the goalkeeper must stand around the near post, facing the ball carrier. His waiting position is low, since he has to handle a situation that is very similar to a 1vs1 "duel" at a close distance, but in this case he has the advantage of knowing where the ball is going to be played; for this reason, the keeper must not stand close to the post, but at a certain distance in a slightly advanced position outside the post. Taking a position in front of the post and not parallel to it helps the goalkeeper save corner kicks or possible, but very unlikely, shots at goal, while avoiding deflecting the ball into the net. On the other hand, if he takes an excessively advanced position outside the post (two yards, for example) and the attacking opponent near the end line manages to pass the ball to one of his teammates, the goalkeeper has to recover his position inside the goal rapidly while standing outside of it.

3.4 Coaching progression to develop courage

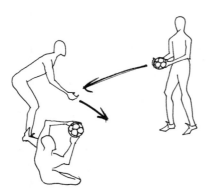

Illustration 10: The coach throws the ball to the goalkeeper from a close distance; at first the keeper saves the ball with a part of his body (for example, his chest, his shoulders, and so on), driving it back to the coach's feet; then, he has to catch the ball before the coach shoots at goal.

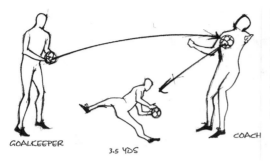

GOALKEEPER   COACH
          3.5 YDS

Illustration 11: The goalkeeper throws the ball at the coach's chest from a distance of about 3 to 4 yards; then, he comes out and makes a fearless breakaway save before the coach controls the ball with his feet or immediately after, thus stopping a possible shot on goal.

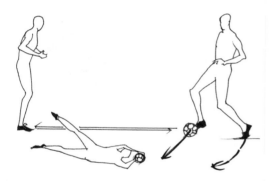

Illustration 12: This exercise is similar to the previous one with the sole variation that the goalkeeper throws the ball to the coach's feet, the coach controls the ball and shoots from a close distance; the keeper tries to catch the ball coming out and make a fearless breakaway save immediately after the coach controls the ball.

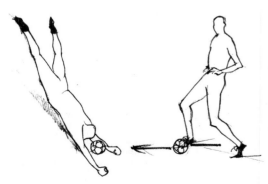

Illustration 13: The goalkeeper tries to intercept the ball without using his arms, stopping the ball with any other part of the body (his head, preferably).

Variation: the exercise can be performed alternating hand saving (the proper technique) with head saving.

41

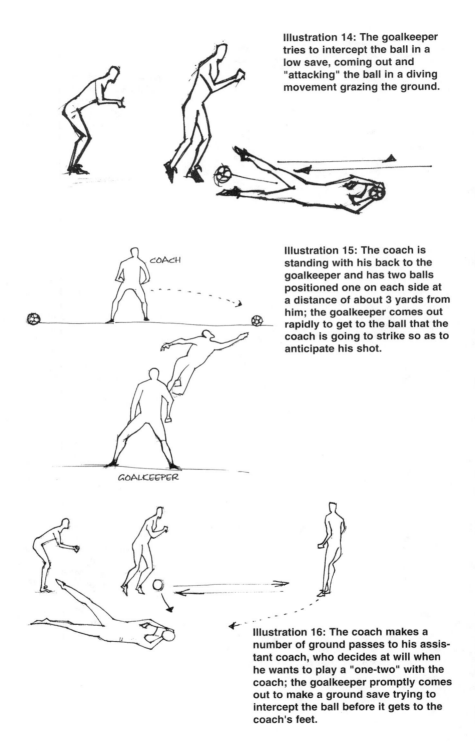

Illustration 14: The goalkeeper tries to intercept the ball in a low save, coming out and "attacking" the ball in a diving movement grazing the ground.

COACH

Illustration 15: The coach is standing with his back to the goalkeeper and has two balls positioned one on each side at a distance of about 3 yards from him; the goalkeeper comes out rapidly to get to the ball that the coach is going to strike so as to anticipate his shot.

GOALKEEPER

Illustration 16: The coach makes a number of ground passes to his assistant coach, who decides at will when he wants to play a "one-two" with the coach; the goalkeeper promptly comes out to make a ground save trying to intercept the ball before it gets to the coach's feet.

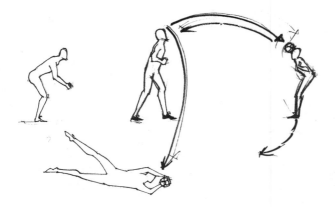

Illustration 17: This exercise is similar to the previous one with the sole variation that the coach and the assistant make head passes; in this case, the goalkeeper comes out to make a fearless mid-height save.

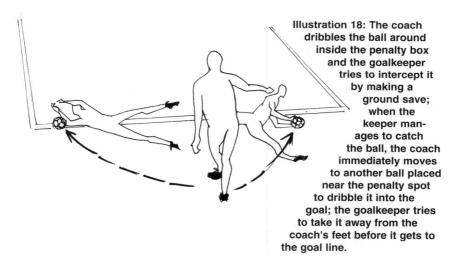

Illustration 18: The coach dribbles the ball around inside the penalty box and the goalkeeper tries to intercept it by making a ground save; when the keeper manages to catch the ball, the coach immediately moves to another ball placed near the penalty spot to dribble it into the goal; the goalkeeper tries to take it away from the coach's feet before it gets to the goal line.

43

3.5   DRILLS
To improve saving technique

Drill n.1

Purpose:

Learn and improve high saving technique.

Procedure:

This exercise simulates a cross coming from the flanks of the field. The coach throws a ball from a close distance that lands in one of the four set areas (see illustration 5 on page XX); the goalkeeper tries to intercept the ball using the techniques explained above.

Number of repetitions:

4-5 crosses per sector before suitable recovery.

Notes:

Performing this exercise the goalkeeper learns to choose his starting position in relation to the ball and to memorize all the steps he has to take before "taking off" for a high save. The coach's job is to correct any mistakes.

Especially suggested for:

All goalkeepers in training sessions focusing on saving technique. It can also be used as a warm up for youth keepers but with fewer repetitions.

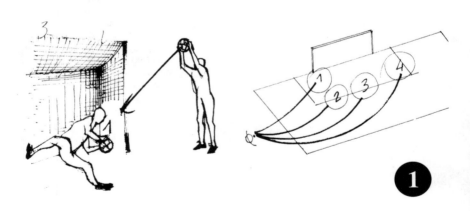

Drill n.2

Purpose:
Improve saving technique and ball path reading.

Procedure:
The coach throws a high ball that lands in the penalty box; before the ball starts its path down, the goal-keeper must place a hoop on ground to mark the zone where the ball is going to land.

Number of repetitions:
6-8 repetitions per sector before suitable recovery.

Notes:
Performing this exercise the goal-keeper learns to read and anticipate the path of the ball and check the right choice.

Especially suggested for:
All goalkeepers in training sessions focusing on saving technique; youth keepers in at any time in their standard training week.

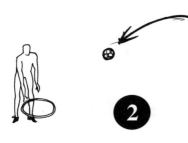

Drill n.3

Purpose:
Improve saving technique and ball path reading.

Procedure:
The coach throws a high ball that lands in the box; the keeper lets the ball bounce and catches it with both hands.

Number of repetitions:
6-8 repetitions before suitable recovery.

Notes:
Performing this exercise the goal-keeper learns to read and anticipate the path of the ball and check the right choice.

Especially suggested for:
All goalkeepers in training sessions focusing on saving technique; it can also be used as warm-up for youth keepers but with fewer repe-titions.

Purpose:
Improve saving technique and ball path reading.

Procedure:
From the flanks of the field the coach throws a ball describing a high path and landing inside the box; the goalkeeper positions exactly where the ball is going to land and catches it with both arms extended upward while standing motionless on the spot.

Number of repetitions:
6-8 repetitions before suitable recovery.

Notes:
Performing this exercise the goalkeeper learns to read and anticipate the path of the ball and check the right choice.

Especially suggested for:
All goalkeepers in training sessions focusing on saving technique; it can also be used as warm-up for youth keepers but with fewer repetitions.

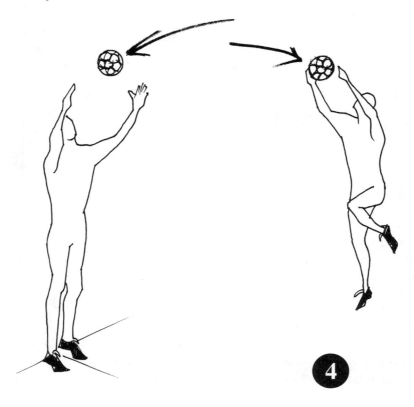

Drill n.5

Purpose:

Improve saving technique and ball path reading.

Procedure:

Inside the penalty box (between the goal area and the penalty spot) mark out five square areas 3-4 yds wide that are called by progressive numbers; the coach throws a ball that will and into one of those squares; the goalkeeper shouts loudly the number of the area where the ball is going to land before it begins its path down.

Variation:

In addition to calling the number of the square where the ball is going to land, the goalkeeper also has to move there and intercept the ball with a high save.

Number of repetitions:

6-8 repetitions before suitable recovery.

Notes:

Performing this exercise the goalkeeper learns to read and anticipate the path of the ball and check the right choice. In the exercise suggested in the variation, the goalkeeper simulates a real game situation where he has to come off the goal line and make a high save.

Especially suggested for:

All goalkeepers in pre-season training sessions focusing on saving technique; youth keepers in the sessions dealing with reading the path of the ball.

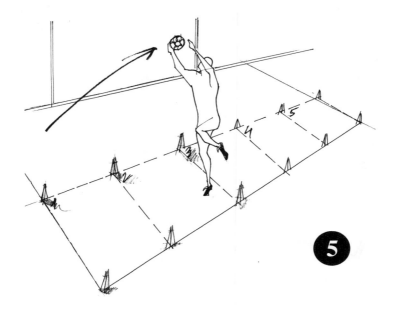

Drill n.6

Purpose:
Improve saving technique and performance speed.

Procedure:
From the flanks of the field the coach throws a ball into the penalty box; before catching the ball, the goalkeeper looks at his teammate standing at the post opposite to the ball, who will hold up a number with his fingers; when the keeper sees the number, he calls it loudly and makes a high save. It is important to remember to call the ball by shouting "mine!" or "keeper!".

Number of repetitions:
6-8 repetitions before suitable recovery.

Notes:
Performing this exercise the goalkeeper learns to come off the goal line and make a high save; reading the number is a way to delay the keeper's action, which forces him to speed up the steps preceding the take-off and consequently move more rapidly. This method simulates rather accurately what really happens in matches and cannot be reproduced perfectly in training sessions by means of a simple crossing exercise.

Especially suggested for:
All goalkeepers in pre-season training sessions focusing on saving technique.

Purpose:
Learn and improve punching technique.

Procedure:
The goalkeeper is standing in the 6-ye box; he throws the ball upward and slightly forward over his head and punches it away towards the coach standing around the penalty spot. The coach catches the ball punched by the goalkeeper and immediately drop kicks it at goal, thus forcing the keeper to make a diving save.

Variation:
The goalkeeper can punch the ball forward using the right hand, the left hand, or both hands together.

Number of repetitions:
4-6 repetitions before suitable recovery.

Notes:
Performing this exercise the goalkeeper learns to punch the ball correctly and then make a save.

Especially suggested for:
All goalkeepers in training sessions focusing on punching technique.

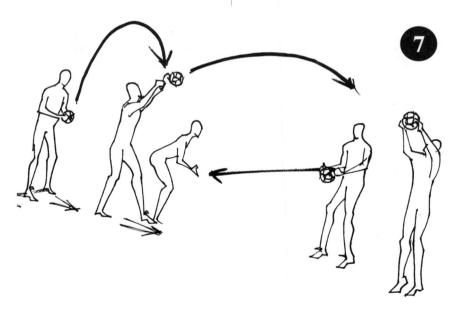

49

Purpose:

Learn and improve punching technique.

Procedure:

An assistant coach is standing near the sideline of the penalty box and throws the ball over the keeper's head to force him to punch the ball to clear it away, prolonging its trajectory.

Variation:

In addition to punching the ball to prolong its trajectory, the keeper also has to position very rapidly and correctly to catch the next shot on goal that the coach takes from the point where the ball lands after being cleared away by the goalkeeper.

Number of repetitions:

4-6 repetitions before suitable recovery.

Notes:

Performing this exercise the goalkeeper learns to punch the ball correctly and then make a save.

Especially suggested for:

All goalkeepers in training sessions focusing on punching technique.

Purpose:
Improve diving technique combined with a punching save.

Procedure:
The coach is standing between the penalty spot and the line of the 6-ye box, with his arms stretched out, holding a ball in each hand; the goalkeeper is standing on the goal line. The coach throws one of the balls upward and the keeper moves to dive and punch it away before it lands on the ground. It is advisable to use two mats placed on each side of the coach as cushions to soften the landing.

Variation:
The goalkeeper can punch the ball forward using the right hand, left hand or both hands together.

Number of repetitions:
4-6 repetitions before suitable recovery.

Notes:
Performing this exercise the goalkeeper learns to punch the ball away correctly.

Especially suggested for:
All goalkeepers in training sessions focusing on punching technique.

4.1 The standard waiting position

Before focusing our attention on diving technique it is important to understand the waiting position preparing for the movement.

The expression "waiting position" refers to the correct "posture" that the goalkeeper should take to start the saving action (diving, in this case).

The correct waiting position varies in relation to the distance between the goalkeeper and the ball. For example, when the ball is far from the goal (30 yards or more), it is advisable for the goalkeeper to take the so-called "high" position (see illustration 1); on the other hand, if the ball is closer to the goal and can be shot at goal easily (from a distance of about 16 to 20 yards), the keeper takes a "mid-height" position (as shown in illustration 2). Finally, when the ball is very close to the goal - like in a 1vs1 "duel" (attacking player vs goalkeeper), the standard waiting position is "low" (see illustration 3).

Illustration 1: When the ball is far from the goal, the goalkeeper takes a "high" waiting position.

Illustration 3: When the ball is very close to the goal - like in a 1vs1 "duel" - the goalkeeper takes a "low" waiting position.

Illustration 2: When the ball is near the goal and can be shot at goal easily (about 16 to 20 yards), the goalkeeper takes a "mid-height" waiting position.

4.2 Considerations on the three waiting positions

The adjectives "high", "mid-height" and "low" waiting positions refer to the position of the center of gravity (point at the level of the pelvis around which the weight is evenly distributed) in relation to the ground.

Moreover, in the three different positions the lower limbs are bent at different angles (which causes the weight to be differently distributed on the knee and ankle joints):

-   from about 180° to 170° in the high position;
-   from about 110° to 90° in the mid-height position;
-   from about 35° to 45° in the low position.

In the so-called high posture, less power can be generated (pushing angles are wide open), but the goalkeeper can make nimbler and quicker movements sideways and forward; in the other two waiting positions, the angles at which the legs are bent are closer, which allows the keeper to generate more power when pushing into the dive.

In all three waiting positions the body weight is distributed on the legs - more on the toes than on the heels - and the trunk is bent slightly forward; in the high and mid-height positions, the forearms are parallel to the ground, while in the low position they are at the sides, stretched out with the palms wide open, almost as if they were touching the ground (as shown in illustration 3).

The leg position (i.e. the distance between the two feet) is a rather common mistake that can be easily noticed in the high and mid-height waiting positions; in fact, many times they are too wide apart or too close together, which obviously prevents body balance. In general, it is advisable to open the legs to shoulder width.

By contrast, in the lower position - typical of 1vs1 situations - it is convenient to open the legs wider apart than the shoulders immediately before the shot on goal is taken so as to keep greater balance and stability; in this way, the goalkeeper can get to the ground more easily and rapidly if he has to dive to save a ground shot.

It is particularly important for the keeper to keep his legs "open" at the right distance. If the feet are too wide apart, power is lost in the pushing phase, which results in an ineffective technical move. In the case of a shot taken from a distance of about 16 to 20 yards, if the goalkeeper is standing with his legs too wide apart, he will be forced to make quick movements to adjust his waiting position before starting the saving action; this means loss of time and failure in making a successful save.

A still more unfavorable situation occurs when the goalkeeper is standing with one leg slightly in front of the other before the attacking opponent shoots at goal. This irregular position reduces the goalkeeper's capacity to push and "close" forward and does not allow him to "synchronize" his movements with the actions preceding the opponent's shot.

In a situation of that kind it may happen that the goalkeeper moves the advanced leg backward in order to recover the correct position; also in this case the goalkeeper's diving action is considerably delayed since he must first recover his balance before starting the loading and pushing phase.

In the same way, standing with one's legs too close together is a drawback to making a successful save. In this case, the goalkeeper has to make an "extra" movement before making the final technical move.

In short, it is clear that taking the correct waiting position is of critical importance for goalkeepers.

4.3 Diving technique to save mid-air balls

The diving action begins immediately when the goalkeeper understands the direction of the shot; it continues - if there is enough time - with the keeper stepping sideways and moving the inside leg (i.e. the leg closest to the ball direction) sideways and forward; the action ends with the loading phase to generate power in the legs and the following push into the dive. The goalkeeper should take care of never crossing his legs while stepping sideways; in fact, this situation jeopardizes the goalkeeper's balance and causes his body to extend backward in the following diving phase.

During the pushing phase the whole body (head, trunk, arms and hands) must stretch out - in rapid progression - towards the direction of the ball, in perfect synchrony and coordination; it is clear that the flight phase must be oriented and performed diagonally and forward.

During the flight the pushing leg (the one nearest the direction of the ball) must be kept as close to the ground as possible, while the knee of the other leg is brought across the body pointing at the diving direction for additional boost. When the flight ends, the "landing" phase begins with the outside part of the foot, the leg, the outside part of the knee, the thigh and, finally, the hip that will roll on the ground to help cushion the impact. The saving action will end with the keeper bending his elbows close to the hips and his head bent down towards the chest to help the body "curl" on the ball (see diagram 4 on following page).

Illustration 4

A poor diving technique considerably reduces the real effectiveness of the save. For example, if the goalkeeper raises the pushing leg too much, this causes him to lose strength and arch his body excessively during the flight phase; stepping only sideways and not forward inevitably delays the goalkeeper's action when covering the the shot trajectory forward. Although these bad habits may seem mere details, they often prove to be fundamental to avoid being scored against.

4.4   Diving technique to save ground balls

When the attacking opponent takes a ground shot on goal from medium distance (16 to 20 yards, for instance), the goalkeeper takes a sideways step forward with the pushing leg (the one nearest to the ball) and lets himself collapse to the ground, emphasizing the fall while also avoiding "pivoting" on the body to delay the save on the ground. The arms are extended forward and the hand closest to the ground stops the ball, while the other hand completes the catching with the help of the ground. In the technical slang this diving technique is commonly known as the "triple catch save" (see illustration 5 and 6 below).

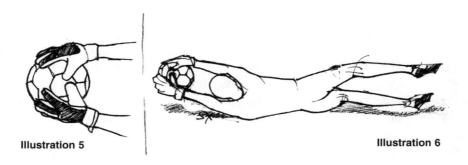

Illustration 5

Illustration 6

4.5   Diving technique to save close-in, unexpected and ground shots

It happens increasingly often during the course of a match that the goalkeeper has to handle a 1vs1 situation to stop the attacking opponent, or to react to save a close-in and unexpected shot, or to find a way out of it in case one of his teammates deflects the ball unintentionally.

In those situations of emergency, the goalkeeper does not have enough time to make the save moving on the trajectory where the ball is coming from, taking quick steps sideways as suggested in the standard saving technique.

In this case, the goalkeeper can intercept the ball in three different manners; in particular he can:

1. Let himself fall on the spot. In order to do that, he must move the leg nearest the ball driving it backward almost as if it were touching the calf of the other leg; this technique helps the trunk fall to the ground almost perpendicularly (see illustration 7).

2. Bend the trunk sideways towards the ball while also moving the legs in the opposite direction, taking short and quick steps.These movements cause the goalkeeper to lose his balance and help him fall to the ground towards the ball (see illustration 8).

3. Move the arms towards the ball before the trunk in order to stop it. This technique allows him to curl on the ball and bring it under control (see illustration 9).

In addition to the techniques mentioned above, it is clear that the instinctive save - made with the feet or any other part of the body - is also effective.

Illustration 7: The goalkeeper drives the left leg (the one nearest the ball) backward almost as if it were touching the calf of the right leg, thus helping him fall to the ground perpendicularly.

Illustration 8: The goalkeeper bends the trunk sideways while also moving the legs in the opposite direction.

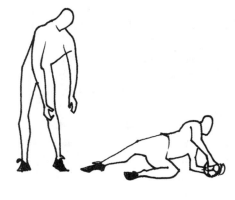

Illustration 9: The goalkeeper moves the arms before the trunk towards the ball in order to stop it and finally curl on the ground.

4.6   Special exercises to improve sideways and forward diving technique

Special attention should be focused on sideways and forward diving technique.

As we already explained in the chapter on "Positioning technique", the goalkeeper should intercept the ball sideways and forward, at the point along the sides of the hypothetical triangle closest to the goalkeeper; in the case of a diving save, those points correspond to the perpendicular lines (see diagram 3 in chapter no.1). Taking the sideways step forward in the wrong way (with the leg nearest the ball) is one of the most common mistakes that goalkeepers make. In fact, even though they have enough time to prepare the diving action correctly, they only take the step sideways, which consequently delays their catching the ball.

This mistake can prove costly, especially in modern soccer where the speed of the performance and even the smallest detail often play a decisive role.

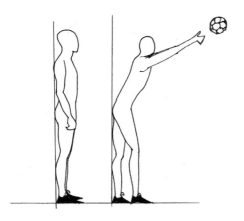

Illustration 10: The goalkeeper is standing in an upright position, with his back and heels touching a wall, he has to intercept the ball, moving only the inside leg in relation to the direction where the ball is coming from. The outside leg must stay on the wall.

Variation: The outside leg will "join" the inside one.

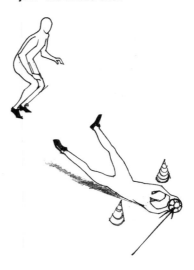

Illustration 11: Starting from the standard waiting position, the goalkeeper performs a sideways dive forward passing between two cones before catching a ground shot. It is advisable to avoid taking too many short steps before diving.

Variation:
The ball can also be thrown to make it bounce on the ground.

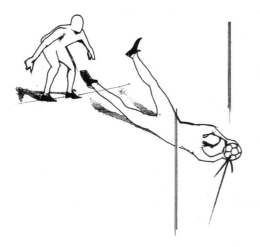

Illustration 12: Starting from the standard waiting position, the goalkeeper makes a sideways dive forward passing between two upright posts before catching a mid-air shot. It is advisable to use a mat to cushion the landing.

Illustration 13: Starting from the standard waiting position in the middle of the goal mouth, the goalkeeper performs a sideways dive forward to head the ball away. It is advisable to use a mat to cushion the landing.

Variation: The exercise can be performed alternating heading with catching saves.

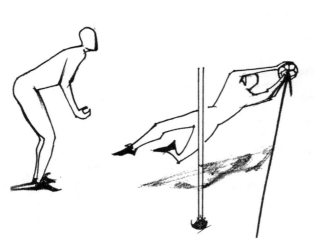

Illustration 14: Starting from the standard waiting position, the goalkeeper has to defend a small-sided goal about four yards wide, placed at a distance of about three yards. The coach is holding two balls, one in each hand, and the ball can be thrown on the ground, in mid-air or with a rebound.

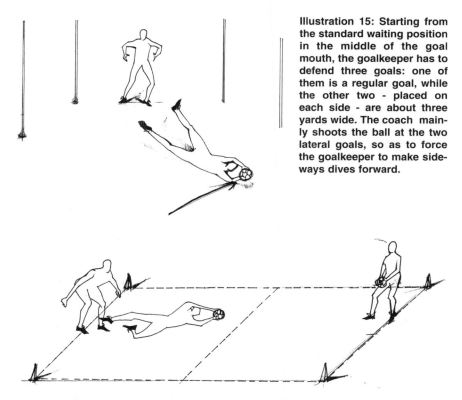

Illustration 15: Starting from the standard waiting position in the middle of the goal mouth, the goalkeeper has to defend three goals: one of them is a regular goal, while the other two - placed on each side - are about three yards wide. The coach mainly shoots the ball at the two lateral goals, so as to force the goalkeeper to make sideways dives forward.

Illustration 16: Mark out two square areas five yards wide having one side in common; two goalkeepers are standing behind the end line and try to intercept the ball thrown by one of their teammates before it bounces on the ground.

Variation: The ball can be caught on the rebound.

4.7   Coaching diving technique to youth goalkeepers

Coaching diving save technique is one of the most important experiences in a youth goalkeeper's training. In fact, this technical move combines several movements together and involves a number of elements including: technique, courage, the pleasure of diving and, furthermore, the ability to "combine" all these elements together.

Consequently, in order to coach this particular technique to youth keepers it is first of all advisable to work out a coaching progression starting from simple exercises and gradually shifting to increasingly complex activities.

Before starting a coaching progression requiring the young goalkeeper to make a diving save and land on the ground, we generally recommend training the player to land on a soft surface, like on a padded mat for example. Landing on such a surface allows the goalkeeper to focus his attention on the purely technical aspect of the save. Moreover, this solution also helps overcome possible fears that may arise in this coaching phase. When this experience has been perfectly internalized, before shifting to the real diving technique it is advisable to train the keeper to gradually "come in contact" with the ground by suggesting a coaching progression starting from simple rolling on the ground and easy pre-acrobatic movements (like turning somersaults forward, backward, while jumping, and so on) to end with the complete diving technique.

4.8 Coaching progression to coach diving technique to youth goalkeepers

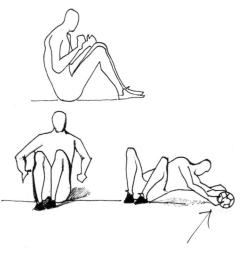

Illustration 17: Starting from a sitting position, with both legs and arms bent, the goalkeeper falls on one side and tries to catch the ball thrown by the coach; the legs remain in the starting position.

Variation: the ball can be thrown both on the ground or in mid-air.

Illustration 18: Starting from a sitting position, with both legs and arms bent, the goalkeeper tries to deflect the ball after it bounces on the ground; the legs help the body stretch out, moving in the opposite direction.

Variation: the ball can also be thrown in mid-air; in this case, the legs make greater effort to help the movement.

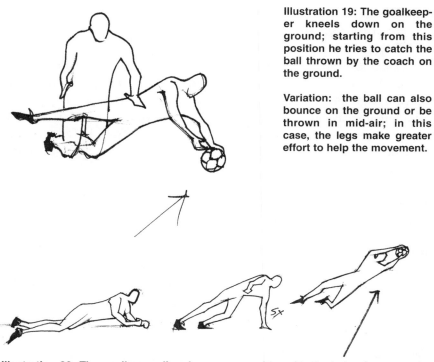

Illustration 19: The goalkeeper kneels down on the ground; starting from this position he tries to catch the ball thrown by the coach on the ground.

Variation: the ball can also bounce on the ground or be thrown in mid-air; in this case, the legs make greater effort to help the movement.

Illustration 20: The goalkeeper lies down on one side; with the help of one arm he gets up and, after taking short steps, makes a dive to catch the ball thrown by the coach.

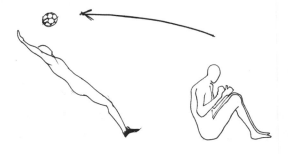

Illustration 21: Starting from a sitting position, with both legs and arms bent, the goalkeeper pushes backward on his legs to try to catch the ball that the coach throws over his head.

Variation: the ball can also be thrown sideways from the right or from the left.

One of the main goals of this coaching progression is to gradually train the youth keeper to learn and internalize all the real movements characterizing the diving save.

Furthermore, this series of exercises can also be used to train adult keepers to "come in contact" with the ground, especially in the pre-season training phase when both summer rest and hard grounds generally make the impact with the ground more difficult.

4.9 DRILLS
To improve diving technique

Situational training (which means the technical move introduced in a real game situation) proves to be the most successful and effective means to learn and internalize all the techniques peculiar to each position, including goalkeeper. If in the training sessions you are able to reproduce the events and situations occurring in the course of a match (for example, more or less dangerous attacking maneuvers) while also combining them with a level of attention, concentration and state of mind similar to a competition, the goalkeeper will get used to identifying the dynamics of the playing actions and be "ready" to anticipate them. Performing situational training the goalkeeper learns to understand whether the opponents' action will cause danger by reading the smallest details (the opponents' disposition on the field, the position of the ball, whether the opposition are likely to shoot at goal or not, an so forth); in this way, he is able to anticipate any possible consequence. The ability to understand and anticipate how playing actions will develop is also useful in judging shooting opportunities successfully; how many times do field players tell their goalkeeper that he could have saved such a goal: "why didn't you understand that he was going to shoot left?!". In fact, before taking a shot on goal the ball carrier always makes some preparatory movements with his body which can help the goalkeeper (who is used to this training method) understand the direction, the speed and the type of shot that the opponent is going to take; it is clear that being able to "read" this situation obviously helps the goalkeeper prepare his defensive action.

This is why it is advisable to train goalkeepers using the coaching method based on real game situations.

If you want to understand if your goalkeeper is able to "read" a situation of play or a final shot on goal, it could be helpful to test his abilities using a videotape where some attacking maneuvers and shots are recorded; you can stop the video before the shot is taken: if the goalkeeper is able to read the situation, this means that he is also able to anticipate the characteristics of the shot.

Drill n.1

Purpose:
Learn and improve diving technique on ground balls and unexpected and close-in shots.

Procedure:
The goalkeeper is standing in the middle of a regular goal and first deflects a ground ball kicked from the edge of the box (16 yds) towards the area around one of the posts; as soon as the keeper deflects the ball, the coach takes another shot off the pass played by his assistant coach standing near the end line outside the goal area.

Number of repetitions:
4-5 repetitions before suitable recovery.

Notes:
Performing this exercise the goalkeeper learns to deflect the ball into a corner kick and - in case he fails (as is shown in this example) - to catch a second shot that the opponent could take as a result of the keeper's poor deflection.

This exercise also trains the keeper to take the best position to save the second unexpected shot very quickly; the more rapidly the keeper gets up after making the first save, the more likely he is to catch the second shot.

Especially suggested for:
All goalkeepers in training sessions dealing with real game situations.

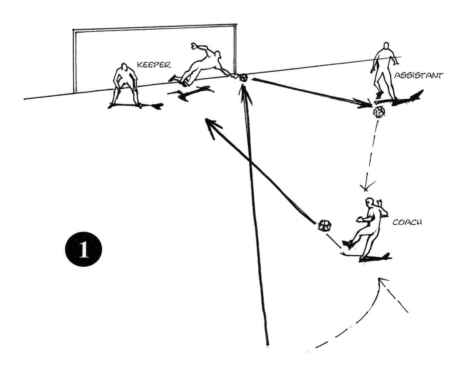

65

Drill n.2

Purpose:

Learn and improve diving technique.

Procedure:

The goalkeeper throws the ball against the crossbar to simulate a situation where the ball is cleared back; the coach gets possession and takes a shot on goal. The goalkeeper recovers his position in the goal and tries to save the shot.

Variation:

In order to simulate a situation where the ball rebounds off the post, an assistant coach throws the ball from a close distance against the post, forcing the goalkeeper to dive and quickly get up to catch the shot resulting from the rebound against the post.

Number of repetitions:

4-5 repetitions before suitable recovery.

Notes:

Performing this exercise the goalkeeper learns to get up rapidly immediately after making a dive, to come out at the right time at the opponent's feet (if possible), to take up the best position in relation to the ball and to save close in shots.

Especially suggested for:

All goalkeepers in training sessions dealing with real game situations.

2

Variation

66

Purpose:

Learn and improve diving technique.

Procedure:

The goalkeeper positions around the near post and deflects into the penalty box a ground cross made by the assistant coach from the end line; the coach intercepts the ball cleared back by the keeper and shoots at goal; the keeper must recover quickly to save the shot.

Number of repetitions:

4-5 repetitions before suitable recovery.

Notes:

Performing this exercise the goalkeeper learns to react to and save balls coming from the endline and to catch the possible second shot as a result of a poor deflection. This exercise also helps improve performance speed on the second unexpected shot; the quicker the keeper gets up after making the initial save, the more likely he is to catch the second shot.

Especially suggested for:

All goalkeepers in training sessions dealing with real game situations.

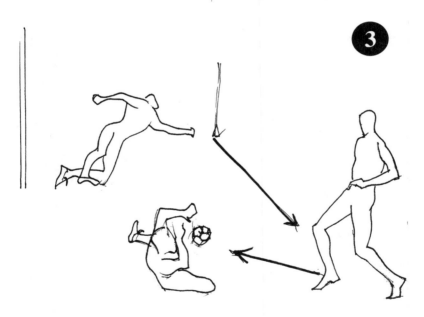

Drill n.4

Purpose:

Learn and improve diving technique.

Procedure:

The goalkeeper positions behind a small-sided goal 4 yds wide and, when the coach gives the signal, he sprints in front of the goal, ready to catch a shot taken from a distance of about 6-7 yds.

Number of repetitions:

5-6 shots before suitable recovery.

Notes:

Performing this exercise the goalkeeper learns to stand in the standard waiting position as long as possible and avoid "sitting down" too soon; this also helps him internalize the diving technique to save unexpected and close-in shots in a situation of play that can develop rather often during the course of a match, especially if his team applies the offside tactical strategy.

Especially suggested for:

All goalkeepers in training sessions dealing with real game situations.

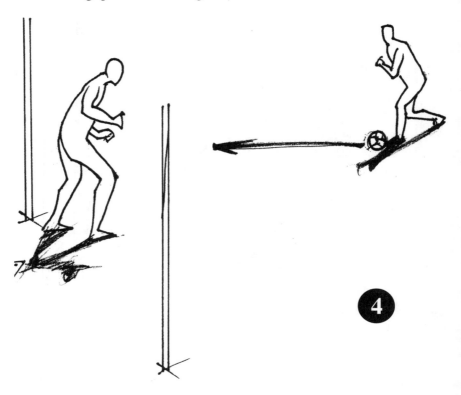

Drill n.5

Purpose:

Learn and improve diving technique to save close-in, ground and also mid-air shots.

Procedure:

The goalkeeper positions behind a small-sided goal 4 yds wide and, when the coach gives the signal, he sprints in front of the goal, ready to catch the shot taken by the coach from a distance of about 6-7 yds; the coach has two balls to choose from when taking the shot and the goalkeeper must be prepared for either ball.

Variation:

Instead of kicking the ball, the coach can throw one of the two balls.

Number of repetitions:

5-6 shots before suitable recovery.

Notes:

Performing this exercise the goalkeeper learns to stand in the standard waiting position as long as possible and avoid "sitting down" too soon; this also helps him internalize the diving technique to save unexpected and close-in shots on along the ground or in the air in a situation that can develop rather often during the course of a match, especially if his team applies the offside tactical strategy.

Especially suggested for:

All goalkeepers in training sessions dealing with real game situations.

69

Purpose:
Learn and improve diving technique to save close-in shots, tactical sense, positioning technique and performance speed.

Procedure:
The goalkeeper positions around the near post, facing the opponent in possession of the ball standing near the end line inside the penalty box; the ball carrier passes the ball into the box towards the coach, who takes a shot on goal with his own ball before shooting the ball coming from the end line. After saving the first shot, the keeper must immediately reposition to make the second save.

Number of repetitions:
6-7 before suitable recovery.

Notes:
In this simulation of play the goalkeeper learns to make a prompt dive to try to save a close-in shot. In addition to the basic technical moves, this complex exercise also helps stimulate speed of movements, reaction capacity and , in particular, the abilities of perception and analysis like the ability to time one's action, control one's body and obviously the ability to combine all these elements together in the final saving action. One of the most frequent mistakes that goalkeepers generally make in this exercise is to lose their balance backward, almost "sitting down" and simply trusting to chance.

Especially suggested for:
All goalkeepers in training sessions dealing with real game situations.

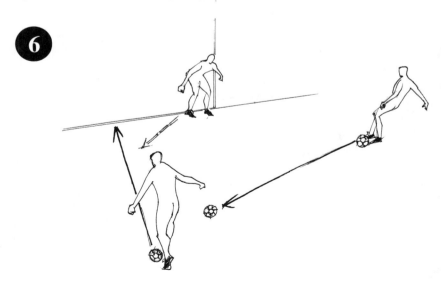

Drill n.7

Purpose:
Learn and improve diving technique.

Procedure:
The goalkeeper positions around the near post, facing the opponent in possession of the ball standing near the end line inside the penalty box; the ball carrier gives a ground pass to his two attacking teammates (n.1 and n.2) standing inside the penalty area; they promptly move to get to the ball, one at the near post and the other at the far post. One of them shoots at goal (they have previously decided who will shoot) while the other makes a feint.

Number of repetitions:
4-5 before suitable recovery.

Notes:
In this simulation of play the goalkeeper learns to anticipate the attacker and make a ground save at his feet, to position inside the goal quickly (if he has decided that it is not advisable to come out) to try to catch any possible shot that the attacker at the near post could take from close in and also to take up the best position in case the attacking opponent n.2 makes a feint and shoots at goal. In addition to the basic technical moves, this exercise helps stimulate speed of movements, reaction capacity and, above all, the abilities of perception and analysis, like the ability to time one's action, control one's body and combine all these elements together in the final save.

Especially suggested for:
All goalkeepers in training sessions dealing with real game situations.

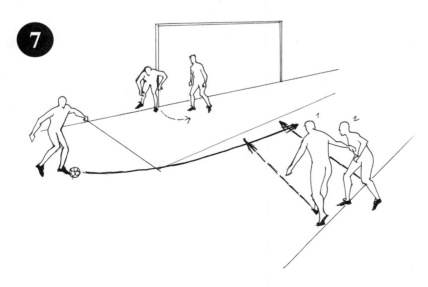

71

Drill n.8

Purpose:
Learn and improve diving technique.

Procedure:
The goalkeeper positions in the middle of a standard goal, focusing his attention on the opponent in possession of the ball (n.1) who is standing near one of the two top corners of the penalty box; player n.1 passes the ball to his teammate n.2, who moves towards him to play a wall-pass with player n.3 standing in a central position at a distance of about 18-20 yds from the goal line. Player n.3 takes a first-touch shot on goal.

Number of repetitions:
4-5 before suitable recovery.

Notes:
Performing this exercise the goalkeeper not only practices the diving technical move but also learns to take up the best advance position to cover the attacker's shooting angle. Furthermore, this situational exercise also helps the goalkeeper understand the opponent's rhythm of action and thus "synchronize" his action with that rhythm, making the most useful movements to execute a successful save.

Especially suggested for:
All goalkeepers in training sessions dealing with real game situations.

72

Drill n.9

Purpose:
Learn and improve diving technique.

Procedure:
The goalkeeper positions in the middle of a standard goal, focusing his attention on the opponent in possession of the ball (n.1) who is standing near one of the two top corners of the penalty box; player n.1 plays One-Two at pace with one of his teammates and subsequently passes the ball to another teammate who is breaking through into the box from the opposite corner to shoot at goal.

Number of repetitions:
4-5 before suitable recovery.

Notes:
In addition to practicing the diving technique to save close-in shots, the goalkeeper also learns to read a situation of play that can develop rather frequently during a match.

Especially suggested for:
All goalkeepers in training sessions dealing with real game situations.

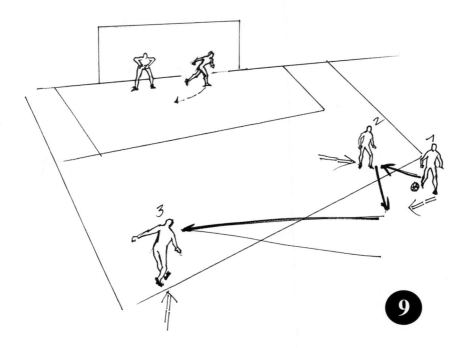

Drill n.10

Purpose:

Learn and improve diving technique, tactical sense and saving technique.

Procedure:

The goalkeeper positions in the middle of a standard goal, focusing his attention on the opponent in possession of the ball (n.1) who is standing in a central position at a distance of about 20 yds from the goal line; another teammate (n.2) is standing at the edge of the box, he moves towards the ball carrier (n.1) and plays a wall pass with a third teammate, who rapidly makes a diagonal pass to the outside attacking player (n.4) who is breaking through into the box to shoot at goal. In this exercise, when player n.2 moves towards his teammate to play a wall pass, the keeper must move upward at the line of the 6-ye box in order to make a ground save or intercept any ball played in depth to the outside attacking opponents. In order to make the exercise easier to perform, it is possible to reduce the number of players involved in the offensive maneuver (from 4 to 2) providing that all the passes are given at the right time; furthermore, in order to simulate a 4-player defensive line it is possible to use four upright posts acting as defenders.

Number of repetitions:

4-5 before suitable recovery.

Notes:

In addition to practicing the diving technique to save close-in shots, the goalkeeper also learns to read a situation of play that can develop rather frequently during a match.

Especially suggested for:

All goalkeepers in training sessions dealing with real game situations.

74

Purpose:

Learn and improve diving technique to save close-in shots.

Procedure:

The goalkeeper positions in the middle of a standard goal, focusing his attention on the opponent in possession of the ball (n.1) who is standing inside the penalty box near one of the two sidelines; player n.1 dribbles the ball outward and finally shoots at goal.

Variation:

Player n.1 can also dribble the ball inside and shoot. *(note: 2 upright posts can be used to simulate the defending opposition)*

Number of repetitions:

6-7 before suitable recovery.

Notes:

Performing this exercise the goalkeeper also learns to constantly keep his eyes on the ball and make a save either diving or not, using not only his technical skills and/or his physical attributes, but also other important qualities like courage, self-control and the ability to take the best decision before acting. One of the most frequent mistakes that goalkeepers generally make when performing this exercise is to lose their balance and put their weight backward, thus bringing their buttocks near the ground and simply trusting to chance.

Especially suggested for:

All goalkeepers in training sessions dealing with real game situations.

According to K. Meinel, the term "agility" refers to the "capacity to carry out fine motor tasks rapidly and adequately in relation to the final goal". (Teoria dell'allenamento - "The theory of training" note of the translator - Società Stampa Sportiva - Roma). The German author uses the adjective fine to define a motor action that is performed in a small space and with little power involved, but with great rapidity and accuracy of the hands, fingers and feet.

As far as goalkeepers are concerned, the term agility simply refers to their ability to constantly master and keep the ball under their control; obviously, this quality cannot be compared to the skills of a juggler in a circus, but can neither refer to the ability of a player handling the ball in a clumsy and inaccurate manner.

Consequently, refined / fine agility can prescind neither from muscle differentiation, which means the capacity to control muscle contraction in relation to the work load and the activity one has to carry out, nor from refined control of the movements one has to make. Being distinctly agile means that one is able to "harmonize" all the movements one has to make in rapid and accurate succession.

If you carefully focus your attention on the movements that a goalkeeper makes in order to decide the best actions to perform before making a save, you realize that both eye-and-hand coordination - that is the relation between eyes and hands to keep control of the upper limbs in relation to the position and the movements of the ball - as well as space-and-time coordination - that allows the player to keep perception and control of the body at any moment and everywhere in space - are of critical importance.

It is useless for a goalkeeper to have great sensibility in his fingers if he can never get to the ball at the right time.

5.1 Training

The goalkeeper can never give up special training to improve his ability to master the ball. In fact, this skill constantly needs to be practiced and refined even when the goalkeeper is a top-class athlete or is at the end of his soccer career.

This means that once a week - at least - it is necessary to stimulate the goalkeeper to concentrate on his agility and his ability to master his moves properly in order to improve ball control.

Finally, remember that it is not fundamental that the keeper performs the exercises perfectly in training sessions, but it is useful that he endeavors to practice with a will, total concentration and care because he must be able to adapt to any situation of play that may develop during the course of a match.

5.2 DRILLS
To improve agility and performance speed

Drill n.1

Purpose:
Learn and improve technical skill; speed up the performance of the diving save.

Procedure:
The goalkeeper dribbles the ball with his hands like in basketball, alternating his left and right hands; when the coach gives the signal, the keeper abandons his ball and intercepts the coach's shot. The coach can decide to kick the ball to force the keeper to make a high catch (in this case, the ball is shot centrally) or a diving save (in this case, the ball is kicked to either side).

Variation n.1:
The keeper passes the ball from one hand to the other in a circular movement around his hips; when the coach gives the signal, he abandons his ball and moves to intercept the coach's shot.

Variation n.2:
The keeper makes the ball pass under his right and left thigh alternately in rapid succession; when the coach gives the signal, the keeper abandons his ball and moves to intercept the coach's shot.

Number of repetitions:
4-6 before suitable recovery.

Notes:
Performing this exercise the goalkeeper develops the proper technical skill to master the ball and speed up the preparatory movements for the save. Both exercises

help stimulate catching skills since the keeper is required to catch the coach's shot despite being in an unfavorable situation as a result of his unstable waiting posture.

Especially suggested for:
All goalkeepers in training sessions focusing on agility.

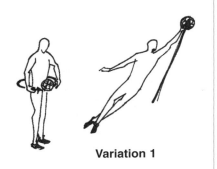

Variation 1

Variation 2

Purpose:
Learn and improve technical skill; speed up the performance of the diving save.

Procedure:
The goalkeeper juggles the ball in the air using the right and left fist

alternately; when the coach gives the signal, the keeper abandons his ball and positions to intercept the coach's shot. The coach can decide to kick the ball to force the keeper to make a high save (in this case he takes a central shot) or a diving save (in this case the ball is kicked to either side).

Variation:
The keeper passes the ball from his right palm to the left one by throwing it over his head; when the coach gives the signal, he abandons his ball and moves to intercept the coach's shot.

Number of repetitions:
4-6 before suitable recovery.

Notes:
Performing this exercise the goal-keeper develops the proper technical skill to master the ball and speed up the preparatory movements for the next save. Both exercises help stimulate catching skills since the keeper is required to catch the coach's shot despite being in an unfavorable position as a result of his unstable waiting posture.

Especially suggested for:
All goalkeepers in training sessions dealing with real game situations.

GOALTENDER

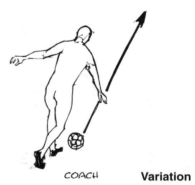

COACH   **Variation**

Drill n.3

Purpose:
Learn and improve technical skill; speed up the performance of the diving save.

Procedure:
The goalkeeper juggles the ball in the air heading it upward; when the coach gives the signal, the keeper abandons his ball and rapidly positions to intercept the coach's shot.

Number of repetitions:
4-6 before suitable recovery.

Notes:
Performing this exercise the goalkeeper learns to control the ball with his head and speed up all the useful movements to make a save. The exercise also stimulates catching skills since the keeper is required to catch the ball to save the coach's shot despite being in an unfavorable position due to his unstable posture.

Especially suggested for:
All goalkeepers in training sessions focusing on agility skills.

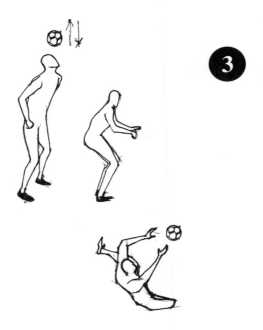

Drill n.4

Purpose:
Learn and improve technical skill; speed up the performance of the diving save.

Procedure:
The goalkeeper throws 2 balls upward; he makes a 360° turn and catches the balls.

Variation:
The goalkeeper performs the exercise we have just described and immediately has to intercept the shot that the coach takes from medium distance.

Number of repetitions:
4-6 before suitable recovery.

Notes:
Performing these exercises the goalkeeper develops the proper technical skill to master the ball and to speed up the preparatory movements to make a save. In both exercises, the keeper finds himself in an unusual position (he does not have any pushing angle) and is forced to speed up the move.

Especially suggested for:
All goalkeepers in training sessions focusing on agility skills.

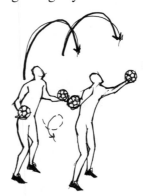

Purpose:

Learn and improve technical agility and catching skills; speed up the performance of the diving save.

Procedure:

The goalkeeper juggles the ball with his feet; when the coach gives the signal, he promptly abandons the ball and tries to save the coach's shot. The coach can decide to kick the ball to force the keeper to make a high catch or a diving save.

Variation:

Instead of using his feet, the goalkeeper can juggle the ball with his thighs.

Number of repetitions:

4-6 repetitions before suitable recovery.

Notes:

Performing this exercise the goalkeeper develops the proper technical skill to master the ball and to speed up the preparatory movements to make a high save.

Especially suggested for:

All goalkeepers in training sessions focusing on agility skills.

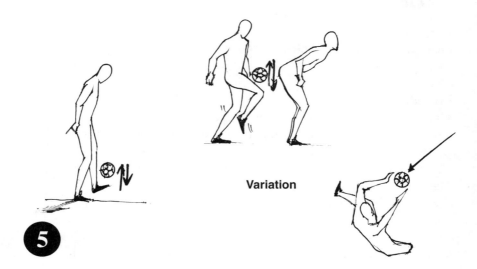

Variation

5

Purpose:
Learn and improve technical agility; speed up the performance of the diving save.

Procedure:
The goalkeeper passes the ball from one hand to the other between his legs at knee height in a figure 8 pattern; when the coach gives the signal, he rapidly abandons his ball and performs a dive to save the coach's shot.

Variation n.1:
The keeper passes the ball from one hand to the other on the ground rather than at mid-height.

Variation n.2:
The keeper juggles two balls like a juggler.

Number of repetitions:
4-6 repetitions before suitable recovery.

Notes:
Performing this exercise the goalkeeper develops the proper technical skill to master the ball, take the right posture and speed up the preparatory movements to make a high save.

Especially suggested for:
All goalkeepers in training sessions focusing on agility skills.

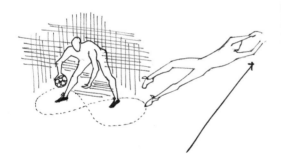

Variation 2

Drill n.7

Purpose:
Learn and improve technical agility; speed up the performance of the diving save.

Procedure:
The goalkeeper bounces the ball on the ground and catches it behind his back before it bounces again; when the keeper catches the ball, the coach immediately takes a shot at goal from medium distance, forcing the keeper to make a diving save.

Variation:
Before catching the ball behind his back, the goalkeeper performs a forward somersault and positions to save the coach's shot.

Number of repetitions:
4-6 repetitions before suitable recovery.

Notes:
Performing this exercise the goalkeeper enhances both space-time perception (accurately reading the ball trajectory) and hand-eye coordination (catching the ball behind his back) and also learns to take up the proper saving position and speed up the movements of his arms as well.

Especially suggested for:
All goalkeepers in training sessions focusing on agility skills.

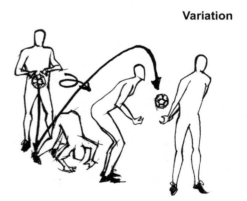

Variation

Purpose:
Learn and improve technical agility; enhance the speed of the performance.

Procedure:
Two goalkeepers are standing 5-6 yds apart facing each other; each one dribbles 2 balls (one for each hand) on the ground; when the coach gives the signal, they throw the 2 balls in a high path and try to intercept the balls thrown by their teammate before they bounce on the ground.

Number of repetitions:
4-6 repetitions before suitable recovery.

Notes:
Performing this exercise the goalkeeper enhances both space-time perception (accurately reading the ball trajectory) and hand-eye coordination (catching both balls).

Especially suggested for:
All goalkeepers in training sessions focusing on agility skills.

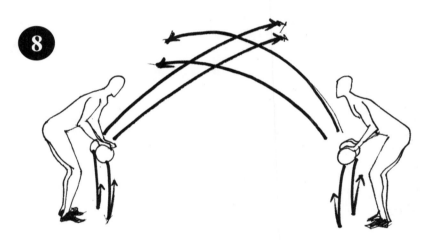

"Catching technique" refers to the goalkeeper's ability to "grasp" and stop the ball using his hands.

Good catching technique allows goalkeepers to break the opposition's attacking maneuver and immediately start their offensive build-up with their team moving upfield.

On the contrary, if a keeper does not have good catching skills and constantly resorts to kicking or punching saves or deflections, he is of little help and may even be dangerous for his team.

From the psychological point of view, playing a goalkeeper who has developed good catching technique certainly inspires a feeling of general confidence and safeness in the entire defensive line and also helps discourage the opposition at the same time.

In order to make a successful catch, not only is it necessary to develop good eye-and-hand coordination, but it is also important to be able to differentiate the muscle tone of the legs, the hands and the fingers as well; in fact, if the goalkeeper makes a catch while keeping his muscles excessively contracted, this will inevitably cause him to lose the ball. The fingers play a key role in the catching action; in fact, they have to absorb the speed of the ball in order to prevent the ball from impacting too violently against the palms of the hands.

6.1 Goalkeeping gloves

The technical evolution of the materials used to manufacture goalkeeping gloves has improved so much that now there are special gloves for each season and for all weather conditions; moreover, modern gloves are made of materials that considerably help the goalkeeper both increase the palm surface making contact with the ball and make the impact with the ball less violent and also prevent the ball from slipping through the hands. Anyway, more than practically helping the keeper when making a save, goalkeeping gloves generally give a feeling of safeness and confidence as well as the sensation that they can provide a better grip. Furthermore, many goalkeepers use little tricks to help them develop the sensation that their gloves can grip better, such as squeezing a few drops of lemon juice or moistening the foams with their saliva.

Even though adult keepers can benefit from using special gloves, it is unadvisable for youth keepers - who still have to learn proper catching techniques - to make excessive use of the gloves, since they reduce the sensibility of their fingers and also prevent them from learning from direct experience what every "apprentice" goalkeeper should know: it is not a pair of gloves that makes a goalkeeper reliable!

6.2   Different catching techniques

There are different methods for making a catching save; the position of the arms and the hands mainly depends on the trajectory of the ball.

- Catching technique to save high balls.

This saving technique is used when the ball describes a high path over the goalkeeper's head; in this case, the arms are extended towards the ball with the elbows slightly open and bent so as to cushion the impact; the hands are positioned so as to form a sort of "shell" to stop and cradle the ball; the thumbs are slightly oblique, nearly touching each other with the index fingers forming a sort of heart turned upside down behind the ball (the "W" or contour catch); the other fingers are slightly apart in order to offer a larger surface to make contact with the ball. Finally, the palms of the hands are positioned square to the ball (see illustrations 1 and 2).

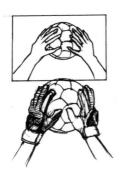

Illustration 1   **Illustration 2**

- Catching technique for shots from about stomach height down.
This cannot be considered a real catching technique, but a special way to position the arms and the hands to direct the ball between the stomach and the knees. This time the arms face downward, with the forearms flat and parallel to the ground, the elbow bent and close to the hips. The palms of the hands face upward and the fingers are slightly open. The

ball is intercepted with the hands first, then it rolls on the forearm and is finally brought up to the chest (see illustrations 3 and 4).

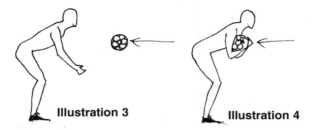

Illustration 3   **Illustration 4**

When the goalkeeper uses this catching save he cannot make the mistake of trying to cushion the shot with his forearms; in fact, unlike the arms, the forearms cannot absorb the energy of the ball, but rather enhance the rebound with the risk of losing control of the ball.

- Catching technique to save shots at about chest height.

In order to make this catch the arms are extended forward, slightly bent, the palms of the hands face upward, the pinkies are very close to each other and the thumbs turn "outward" (see illustration 5).

When making the save the ball first rolls on the hands, then on the forearms that must bend to "cradle" and stop the ball, bringing it up to the chest.

Illustration 5

This catching technique can also be used when the ball is higher or lower than the chest; in those cases, in order to make a clean catch the goalkeeper needs to line up with the shot, either bending or extending his legs.

- Catching technique to save shots at about shoulder height.

In order to make this type of save it is advisable to use the technique that is commonly used to catch high shots; this means that the hands have to stop the ball, the arms bend slightly to absorb the speed of the shot at the same time the catch is made. Then, the ball rolls on the forearms which cradle the ball to hang on to it and bring it up to the chest (see illustration 6).

Illustration 6

- Catching technique to save ground shots.

In order to make this type of save two different catching techniques can be used that differ in the position of the goalkeeper in relation to the direction of the ball.

If the goalkeeper does not need to move to intercept the ground shot, he is forced to bend his trunk from the waist, keeping his legs extended and slightly wide apart (straight-leg pickup), his arms stretched out forward, the hands grazing the ground and the thumbs turning outward. The catch is made with the ball first rolling on the hands and then on the forearms that bend to cradle the ball up to the chest. This catching technique can also be used when the goalkeeper is moving to come out and save shots coming square to him (see illustration 7).

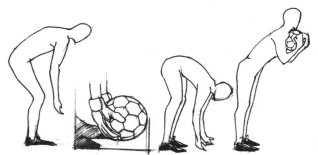

Illustration 7

On the other hand, when the goalkeeper has to move sideways to make a save, the best catching position involves the keeper turning his trunk to face the ball; to catch the ball he bends his legs and the trunk that slightly rotates towards the direction of the ball: this helps the movement of the arms which are stretched out forward to "pick up" the ball.

The goalkeeper bends his legs while running to meet the ball; the leg nearest the ball is bent at the knee and supports the body weight, while the other leg is positioned to form an impenetrable barrier: the knee goes down almost to the ground but should not touch it so that the keeper can easily get up and move in case the ball makes an anomalous rebound or is slightly deflected in some way (see illustration 8).

 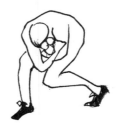

Illustration 8

6.3   DRILLS
To improve catching technique

The exercises that we will show you in the next pages have the main purpose of practicing the different techniques to make catching saves, but they are also useful to improve other technical skills such as agility, diving technique, reaction skill; in fact, every time the goalkeeper gets to the ball, his action always ends with a catching save (with the exception of punching and parrying saves); consequently, all the exercises shown in the chapters focusing on the other technical skills can also be used to train catching technique as well.

Having strong hands and fingers is one of the main characteristics for clean and successful catching.

Therefore, it is advisable for youth goalkeepers in particular - but also for adult keepers - to constantly train their hand muscles; they can use special springs to strengthen their finger flexors or clasp and release suitable tennis or rubber balls.

Drill n.1

Purpose:
Improve catching technique and catching skills.

Procedure:
The goalkeeper is standing on the spot bouncing the ball on the ground; when the coach gives the signal, he promptly stops the ball in his hands in the proper manner.

Variation:
The same as above, but in this case the keeper bounces the ball on the ground while moving around.

Number of repetitions:
10-12 before suitable recovery.

Especially suggested for:
All goalkeepers in training sessions focusing on agility skills.

Drill n.2

Purpose:
Improve catching technique and catching skills.

Procedure:
The coach takes a hard shot at the goalkeeper from a distance of about 12-14 yds; the keeper has to stop the ball using the most suitable catching technique to save the shot.

Variation:
Before intercepting the coach's shot, the goalkeeper turns his head right or left where one of his team-mates is standing. This player raises his arm straight upward and indicates a number with his fingers: the goalkeeper has to repeat that number aloud before catching the shot.

Number of repetitions:
6-8 before suitable recovery.

Especially suggested for:
All goalkeepers in training sessions focusing on catching technique.

Variation

Drill n.3

Purpose:
Improve catching technique and catching skills.

Procedure:
The goalkeeper kicks the ball against a wall from a distance of about 6-8 yds and stops it using the most suitable catching technique in relation to the ball path and direction.

Number of repetitions:
10-12 before suitable recovery.

Especially suggested for:
All goalkeepers in training sessions focusing on catching technique.

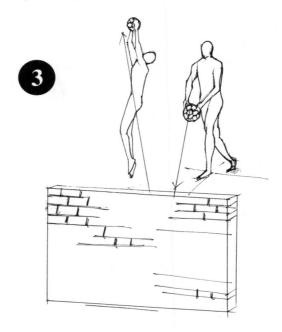

93

Drill n.4

Purpose:
Improve catching technique, catching skills, performance speed and space-time coordination.

Procedure:
The goalkeeper bounces the ball on the ground, turns around and catches the ball using his hands.

Number of repetitions:
6-8 before suitable recovery.

Especially suggested for:
All goalkeepers in training sessions focusing on catching technique.

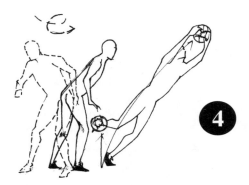

Drill n.5

Purpose:
Improve catching technique, catching skills, performance speed and hand-eye coordination.

Procedure:
The goalkeeper bounces two balls hard on the ground and catches them one after the other. He may need to dive to catch the second before it bounces again.

Number of repetitions:
4-6 before suitable recovery.

Especially suggested for:
All goalkeepers in training sessions focusing on catching technique.

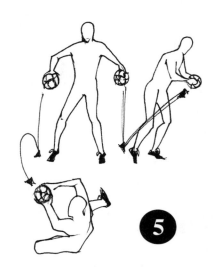

Purpose:
Improve catching technique, catching skills, performance speed and hand-eye coordination.

Procedure:
Three goalkeepers or more position one in front of the other; each one throws a ball up in the air (with the exception of the last one who does not have a ball) and takes off to catch the ball thrown by the teammate standing in front. After throwing the ball, the first keeper in line catches the shot that the coach takes at face height; after making the catch he moves to the end of the line.

Variation:
The goalkeeper throws a ball up and catches a second ball that the coach kicks towards his face; then the keeper throws that ball back to the coach to catch the one he threw up in the air.

Number of repetitions:
4-6 before suitable recovery.

Especially suggested for:
All goalkeepers in training sessions focusing on catching technique.

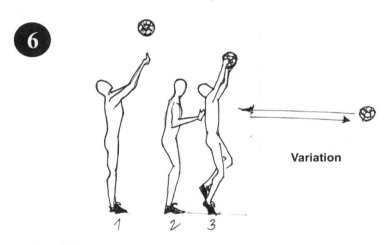

Variation

Purpose:
Improve catching technique, catching skills, performance speed and hand-eye coordination.

Procedure:
Three goalkeepers or more position one in front of the other; each one throws 2 balls up in the air (with the exception of the last one who does not have a ball) and takes off to catch the balls thrown by the teammate standing in front. The first keeper in line catches the shot that the coach takes at face height; after

making the catch he moves to the end of the line.

Variation:
The first goalkeeper also throws 2 balls in the air and must catch and quickly throw back the coach's shot before catching his own balls before they hit the ground.

Number of repetitions:
4-6 before suitable recovery.

Especially suggested for:
All goalkeepers in training sessions focusing on catching technique.

Drill n.8

Purpose:
Improve catching technique, catching skills, performance speed and hand-eye coordination.

Procedure:
The goalkeeper is standing with his back to the coach bouncing a ball hard on the ground; when the coach gives the signal, he promptly turns around to catch and throw back the ball that the coach throws at his face; immediately afterwards, he has to get possession of his own ball (he can make a diving catch) before it bounces again.

Variation:
Instead of throwing the ball with his hands, the coach takes a shot at the keeper's face.

Number of repetitions:
4-6 before suitable recovery.

Especially suggested for:
All goalkeepers in training sessions focusing on catching technique.

Drill n.9

Purpose:
Improve catching technique, catching skills, performance speed and hand-eye coordination.

Procedure:
The goalkeeper bounces the ball on the ground and rapidly positions to catch the shot that the coach takes about chest high. The keeper has to play the ball back to the coach quickly in order to have enough time to catch the ball he was bouncing. He may need to dive to prevent the ball from bouncing again.

Number of repetitions:
4-6 before suitable recovery.

Especially suggested for:
All goalkeepers in training sessions focusing on catching technique.

Drill n.10

Purpose:
Improve catching technique, reaction skills and diving technique.

Procedure:
The goalkeeper throws a ball high in the air and makes a ground save to stop the coach's shot; after deflecting the ball, the keeper gets up quickly to catch the ball he was throwing.

Variation:
The keeper throws a ball up and

dives sideways to catch a ball placed on his right or left; then he quickly gets up to catch the ball he was throwing.

Number of repetitions:
4-6 before suitable recovery.

Especially suggested for:
All goalkeepers in training sessions focusing on catching technique and speed of motion.

○

Drill n.11

Purpose:
Improve catching technique, catching skills and diving technique and stimulate attention.

Procedure:
Two goalkeepers are standing facing each other about 7-8 yds apart and kick the ball back and forth to each other; after striking the ball they have to turn towards the coach who throws or kicks a ball at their face; the keeper stops the ball and plays it back to the coach before receiving the pass from the other keeper.

Variation 1:
Instead of kicking the ball the goal-

keepers throw it to each other and the coach throws a ground ball at their feet.

Variation 2:
The two keepers kick the ball to each other; when the coach call one of their names, that player dives to the right or left, depending on the uncovered side, and tries to make a save.

Number of repetitions:
4-6 before suitable recovery.

Especially suggested for:
All goalkeepers in training sessions focusing on catching technique.

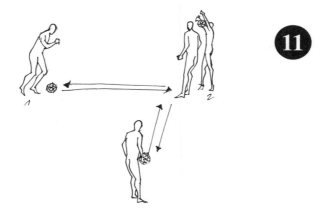

Drill n.12

Purpose:
Improve catching technique, reaction skills and diving technique.

Procedure:
The goalkeeper is standing in front of a wall at a distance of about 5-6 yds and has to catch the ball that the coach standing behind him kicks against the wall.

Variation 1:
Instead of kicking a ground shot, the coach kicks a volley against the wall.

Variation 2:
The goalkeeper is standing facing the coach; when the coach gives the signal, the keeper quickly turns to face the wall and tries to catch the ball that the coach kicks against the wall.

Number of repetitions:
4-6 before suitable recovery.

Especially suggested for:
All goalkeepers in training sessions focusing on catching technique.

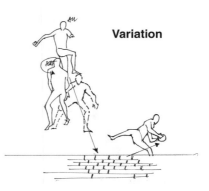

Variation

Reaction skill is a key requirement for soccer goalkeepers; it is often confused with speed of motion, others ascribe mainly unconscious attributes to this skill; now, the most important physiologists define it as a motor-sensorial capacity, pointing out the fact that it combines together perceptive, cognitive and motor elements at the same time. It is clear that any intervention the goalkeeper makes is nothing but a quick response to external needs. At the beginning, the goalkeeper's sensorial receptors perceive the development of the opposition's maneuver (Perception); then, all the components involved in the opposition's play scheme are carefully analyzed, including intentions, chances of success and possibilities of disturbing his team's defensive play (Analysis). For a better perception of the events the athlete's level of attention and concentration is absolutely important, since being able to supervise the situation acts as a selective filter letting only pertinent signs "pass through". Moreover, it is also worthy to remember that "perception" is based on collecting a certain number of sensitive and sensorial stimuli, while "analysis" is based on the goalkeeper's personal capacity to understand them. The analysis is followed by the mental processing of the motor response (Planning). The decision on how to react is favored by "memory", that is nothing but a multitude of events, real life, technical and tactical memories, past experiences one has lived in matches and practice sessions that will help the goalkeeper to choose the best motor response. For this reason, situational training is also important.

The goalkeepers should be incited not only to perform a particular technical move but also to perceive, analyze, remember, anticipate, plan, value the results and finally be able to use them again in the future through a precise coaching program. Furthermore, the coach's job is also to educate the goalkeeper to keep his level of attention and concentration high and, above all, to encourage him to be always highly motivated in order to read and interpret the information he gets from the action in progress so as to provide the most suitable motor response.

The time between the onset of a "stimulus" and the occurrence of the overt "response" to that stimulus is called "response latency". The time the goalkeeper takes to perform the technical move is defined as "rapidity of action" and is part of the general coordination skills and, in particular, of eye-and-hand coordination, which is the ability to combine a "manual" gesture with a visual stimulus. Consequently, the final saving action is nothing but the combination of several elements going from the perception of a stimulus to the performance of the technical move, or better the motor response time.

As you can understand, the goalkeeper's cognitive process is rather complex. Anyway, what we are really interested in is to improve those cognitive processes through "situational" training, while also refining the correct performance and automatization of the various technical moves at the same time. In order to achieve this goal it is important to train leg explosiveness and repeat the exercises at top speed so as to learn to perform them in synchrony with the opponent's action (synchronization).

Finally, it is advisable to remember that training quick reactions should be done in condition of mental freshness; in fact, performing those exercises in a condition of fatigue you simply detach from what really happens during a match.

7.1   DRILLS
To improve reaction skill

Drill n.1

Purpose:
Improve reaction skill and performance speed.

Procedure:
The coach is standing at a distance of about 1 ye from the goalkeeper and throws him a ball just above his head; if the coach calls an uneven number (three, for example), the keeper stops the ball using his hands; by contrast, if the coach calls an even number (two, for instance), the keeper heads the ball back to the coach.

Number of repetitions:
8-10 to be performed in conditions of mental freshness.

Notes:
Performing this exercise the goalkeeper learns to keep concentration as long as possible and to respond to an external stimulus in a rapid and suitable manner. Moreover, it stimulates and monitors the keeper's state of vigilance.

Especially suggested for:
All goalkeepers in training sessions aimed at stimulating attention, reaction speed and speed of motion.

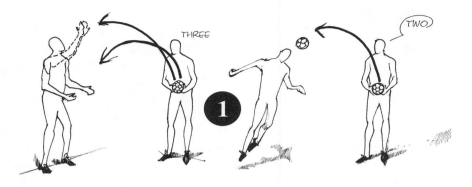

THREE

TWO

Drill n.2

Purpose:
Improve reaction skill and performance speed.

Procedure:
The coach is standing at a distance of about 1 ye from the goalkeeper with two balls, one in each hand (ball n.1 and ball n.2); he bangs the two balls against each other and immediately calls the number of the ball that the keeper has to catch by making a diving save.

Number of repetitions:
5-6 to be performed in conditions of mental freshness. If this exercise is performed the day before a match, it is advisable to do only 2-3 reps.

Notes:
Performing this exercise the goalkeeper learns to keep concentration as long as possible and to respond to an external stimulus in a rapid and suitable manner. Moreover, it stimulates and monitors the keeper's state of vigilance.

Especially suggested for:
All goalkeepers in training sessions aimed at stimulating attention, reaction speed and speed of motion.

ONE

Purpose:

Improve reaction skill and performance speed.

Procedure:

Two goalkeepers position in the middle of the goal, one in front of the other, about 2-3 yds apart, and are called keeper n.1 and keeper n.2 The coach is standing at a distance of about 16-20 yds; just before kicking the ball he calls the number of the keeper who will have to save the shot.

Number of repetitions:

5-6 to be performed in conditions of mental freshness.

Notes:

Performing this exercise the goalkeeper learns to keep concentration as long as possible and to respond to an external stimulus in a rapid and suitable manner. Moreover, it stimulates and monitors the keeper's state of vigilance. In this situation the keeper cannot anticipate the coach's shot following all the preparatory movements, because he does not know whether the coach will call him to make the save or not.

Especially suggested for:

All goalkeepers in training sessions aimed at stimulating attention, reaction speed and speed of motion.

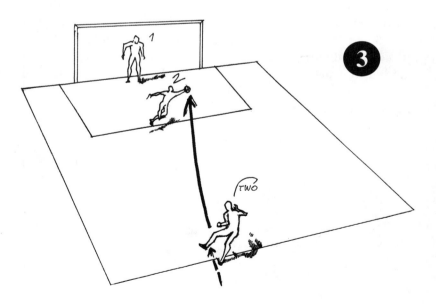

Purpose:
Improve reaction skill and performance speed.

Procedure:
Two coaches are standing facing each other about 3-4 yds apart and make passes inside the penalty box; the coach that will shoot at goal is standing at the edge of the box, while the other is on the penalty spot with his back to the goalkeeper. After making one or more short passes the coach facing the keeper takes a quick shot on goal.

Number of repetitions:
5-6 per goalkeeper, to be performed in conditions of mental freshness.

Notes:
Performing this exercise the goalkeeper learns to keep concentration as long as possible and to respond to an external stimulus in a rapid and suitable manner. Moreover, it stimulates and monitors the keeper's state of vigilance. In this situation the keeper can understand the coach's intentions by reading the movements he makes before shooting.

Especially suggested for:
All goalkeepers in training sessions aimed at stimulating attention, reaction speed and speed of motion.

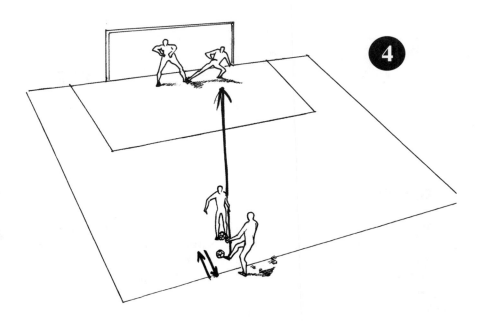

Drill n.5

Purpose:
Improve reaction skill and performance speed.
Procedure:
The goalkeeper throws two balls in the air, spins and catches them.
Variation:
The keeper juggles the ball making head passes with the coach, who is standing about 3-4 yds away. The coach can decide to head the ball back or throw the ball at goal. If he throws the ball at goal, the keeper takes off to prevent the ball from entering the net.

Number of repetitions:
5-6 per goalkeeper, to be performed in conditions of mental freshness.
Notes:
Performing this exercise the goalkeeper learns to keep concentration as long as possible and to respond to an external stimulus in a rapid and suitable manner. Moreover, it stimulates and monitors the keeper's state of vigilance.
Especially suggested for:
All goalkeepers in training sessions aimed at stimulating attention, reaction speed and speed of motion.

Drill n.6

Purpose:
Improve reaction skill and performance speed.
Procedure:
The goalkeeper is standing at a distance of about 3-4 yds from the coach; he throws the ball at the face of the coach, who rapidly throws it

back, trying to take the goalkeeper by surprise. The keeper tries to prevent the coach from scoring.
Number of repetitions:
5-6 per goalkeeper, to be performed in conditions of mental freshness.
Notes:
Performing this exercise the goal-

keeper learns to keep concentration as long as possible and to respond to an external stimulus in a rapid and suitable manner. Moreover, it stimulates and monitors the keeper's state of vigilance.

Especially suggested for:
All goalkeepers in training sessions aimed at stimulating attention, reaction speed and speed of motion.

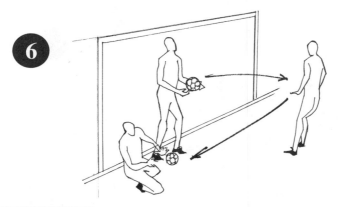

Drill n.7

Purpose:
Improve reaction skill and performance speed.

Procedure:
The goalkeeper and the coach are standing 3-4 yds apart; the keeper throws two balls at the coach's face and the coach only throws one of the two balls back, trying to take the goalkeeper by surprise. The goalkeeper must react quickly to make the save.

Number of repetitions:
5-6 per goalkeeper, to be performed in conditions of mental freshness.

Notes:
Performing this exercise the goalkeeper learns to keep concentration as long as possible and to respond to an external stimulus in a rapid and suitable manner. Moreover, it stimulates and monitors the keeper's state of vigilance. Using two balls makes the situation more difficult for the goalkeeper to handle, since he has to increase his level of attention for the exercise to be successful.

Especially suggested for:
All goalkeepers in training sessions aimed at stimulating attention, reaction speed and speed of motion.

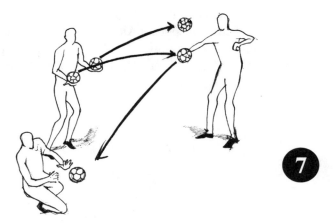

Drill n.8

Purpose:
Improve reaction skill and performance speed.

Procedure:
The goalkeeper and the coach are standing 6-8 yds apart; the keeper throws the ball on the ground to his coach, who takes a first time shot on goal, trying to take the keeper by surprise. The keeper must react quickly to make the save.

Variation:
The keeper throws two balls on the ground to the coach instead of one and the coach only shoots one of them at the goal.

Number of repetitions:
5-6 per goalkeeper, to be performed in conditions of mental freshness.

Notes:
Performing this exercise the goalkeeper learns to keep concentration as long as possible and to respond to an external stimulus in a rapid and suitable manner. Moreover, it stimulates and monitors the keeper's state of vigilance. Using two balls helps increase the difficulty for the keeper, who must increase his level of attention to handle the situation successfully.

Especially suggested for:
All goalkeepers in training sessions aimed at stimulating attention, reaction speed and speed of motion.

8

Drill n.9

Purpose:
Improve reaction skill and performance speed.

Procedure:
Two goalkeepers are standing 7-8 yds apart, each defending his own small-sized goal (about 5-6 yds wide); when the coach gives the signal, each one throws his ball to the teammate standing in front, trying to take him by surprise.

Number of repetitions:
5-6 per goalkeeper, to be performed in conditions of mental freshness.

Notes:
Performing this exercise the goalkeeper learns to keep concentration as long as possible and to respond to an external stimulus in a rapid and suitable manner. Moreover, it stimulates and monitors the keeper's state of vigilance. Making the two goalkeepers challenge one another increases the purpose and the final success of the exercise.

Especially suggested for:
All goalkeepers in training sessions aimed at stimulating attention, reaction speed and speed of motion.

9

109

Drill n.10

Purpose:

Improve reaction skill and performance speed.

Procedure:

Two goalkeepers are standing about 5-6 yds apart, each one defending his own small goal (5-6 yds wide); they make passes heading the ball to one another; when the coach calls one of their names, the keeper that has been called shoots at goal to try to beat his teammate and score a goal.

Number of repetitions:

5-6 per goalkeeper, to be performed in conditions of mental freshness.

Notes:

Performing this exercise the goalkeeper learns to keep concentration as long as possible and to respond to an external stimulus in a rapid and suitable manner. Moreover, it stimulates and monitors the keeper's state of vigilance. Making the two goalkeepers challenge one another increases the purpose and the final success of the exercise.

Especially suggested for:

All goalkeepers in training sessions aimed at stimulating attention, reaction speed and speed of motion.

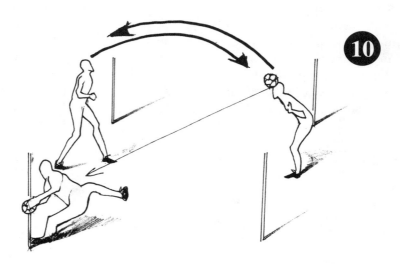

Drill n.11

Purpose:

Improve reaction skill and performance speed.

Procedure:

Two goalkeepers (A and B) are standing outside of a 10 ye wide square area; at each corner of the square there is a ball (the four balls are called n.1, n.2, n.3 and n.4). The goalkeepers skip into the square from any of the four sides; the coach shouts the number of the ball that keeper A has to attack making a quick ground save; at the same time goalkeeper B also moves to attack the ball place diagonally. For example, if the coach calls ball n.1 for goalkeeper A, goalkeeper B promptly moves to catch ball n.3 at the same time.

Number of repetitions:

5-6 per goalkeeper, to be performed in conditions of mental freshness.

Notes:

Performing this exercise the goalkeeper learns to keep concentration as long as possible and to respond to an external stimulus in a rapid and suitable manner. Moreover, it stimulates and monitors the keeper's state of vigilance as well as his speed at understanding what he has to do in a short time.

Especially suggested for:

All goalkeepers in training sessions aimed at stimulating attention, reaction speed and speed of motion.

111

The role of the goalkeeper in modern soccer is based on the ability to make movements - also in rapid sequence one after the other - that allow him to find and/or restore his balance and the best saving posture.

In fact, it is not so important for goalkeepers to avoid losing their balance (the dynamics of their position actually involve moving and losing balance continuously), but it is fundamental that they recover the correct position rapidly.

This means that it is particularly important that the keeper is able to control his body, make acrobatic movements that help him land on the ground in total safety and also face and handle the most varied situations feeling at ease on any occasion. If you consider that goalkeepers are usually rather tall athletes (average height is about 6'1") and that they can also be less agile and coordinated than shorter players, you can easily understand that training balance and acrobatic skills constantly and continuously becomes of critical importance. Therefore, youth keepers should be able to feel at ease when handling the innumerable dangerous and reckless situations developing in matches, that require them to show good dynamic balance and neuromuscular coordination in addition to a good dose of courage; obviously, you cannot pretend that a goalkeeper has the same coordination as an acrobat, but suitable training must be designed to refine acrobatic skills.

A good coach who wants to work on and enhance his players' balance and acrobatic skills should carefully consider both the lively nature of youth keepers (which often causes them to dive in situations where diving is not necessary) and the character of excessively reflecting and fearful athletes who are always afraid of getting hurt and are consequently inclined not to take any "reckless" initiative. If we think of these two different ways of considering the goalkeeper's position, sometimes we tend to believe that the most lively young keepers will become the best goalkeepers in the future, thus forgetting that both of them could become excellent keepers through different coaching progressions.

8.1 Coaching progression to train balance

A successful coaching progression should be based on the principle of "starting from simple activities and passing through increasingly difficult ones", which means simple exercises (like rolling on the ground, turning somersaults on special mats or keeping one's balance standing on one foot, and so forth), to arrive at performing preacrobatic exercises and, finally, even acrobatic moves with and without the ball.

A simple coaching progression to train and enhance balance in youth goalkeepers can develop as follows:

Exercise A: The goalkeeper keeps a medicine ball in perfect balance on his head, at the beginning standing in a static position and then while moving.

Exercise B: The goalkeeper is standing in an upright position in perfect balance on one leg for 10 seconds, at least. Note: perform this exercise alternating the supporting foot and repeat 4 to 6 times.
Variation: perform the same exercise keeping your eyes closed.

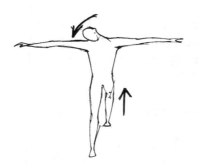

Exercise C: This exercise is similar to the previous one, but this time the keeper bends his head to the shoulder opposite to the raised leg. Note: maintain this position for about 10 seconds, at least, and repeat 4 to 6 times.
Variation: perform the same exercise keeping your eyes closed.

Exercise D: This exercise is similar to the previous one, but in this case the goalkeeper keeps on bending his head on the right and the left shoulder alternately. Note: maintain this position about 10 seconds, at least and repeat 4 to 6 times.
Variation: perform the same exercise keeping your eyes closed.

Exercise E: The goalkeeper performs a somersault forward and stands up on one foot, ready for the central shot the coach is taking. Note: repeat the exercise 4 to 6 times.

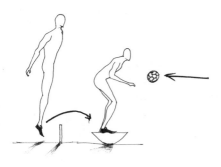

Exercise F: The goalkeeper jumps over a low hurdle with both feet together and lands on an unsteady board trying not to lose his balance. After landing on the board the keeper tries to catch a shot that the coach is taking at his face. Note: perform the exercise 10 to 12 times standing in a frontal position, 10 to 12 times on the right side and 10 to 12 times on the left side. In addition to training balance and catching skills, this exercise helps improve ankle proprioceptive coordination since the player lands on an unsteady surface.

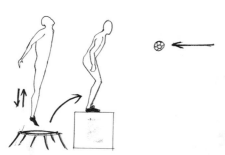

Exercise G: The goalkeeper jumps with both feet together on a springy board and lands on a cube about 12 inches high. After landing on the cube the keeper tries to catch a shot that the coach is taking at his face. Note: Repeat the exercise 7 to 8 times standing in a frontal position, 7 to 8 times on the right side and 7 to 8 times on the left side. In addition to training balance and catching skills, this exercise helps improve ankle proprioceptive coordination in particular when the athlete lands on the cube.

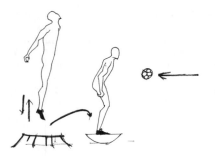

Exercise H: The goalkeeper jumps with both feet together on a springy board and lands on an unsteady board. After landing, the keeper tries to catch a shot that the coach is taking at his face. Note: Repeat the exercise 7 to 8 times standing in a frontal position, 7 to 8 times on the right side and 7 to 8 times on the left side. In addition to training balance and catching skills, this exercise helps improve ankle proprioceptive coordination since the player lands on an unsteady surface.

8.2 DRILLS
To improve balance and acrobatic skills

Drill n.1

Purpose:
Improve the sense of balance.

Procedure:
The goalkeeper positions between the two goal posts with his back to the coach; when the coach gives the signal, the keeper turns to try to catch the shot that the coach takes from the edge of the penalty box.

Number of repetitions:
4-6 before suitable recovery.

Notes:
Performing this exercise the goalkeeper learns to recover his balance quickly after losing it when turning at the coach's signal; this exercise can also help develop catching and diving technique.

Especially suggested for:
All goalkeepers in training sessions designed to work on and improve balance.

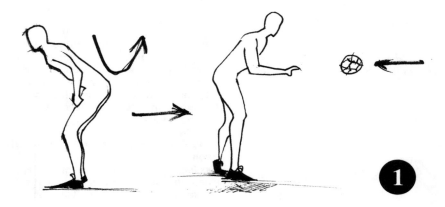

Purpose:

Improve the sense of balance.

Procedure:

The goalkeeper faces the coach; when the coach gives the signal, the keeper turns to try to catch the shot that the coach takes from the edge of the penalty box.

Number of repetitions:

4-6 before suitable recovery.

Notes:

Performing this exercise the goalkeeper learns to recover his balance quickly after losing it when turning at the coach's signal; this exercise can also help develop catching and diving technique.

Especially suggested for:

All goalkeepers in training sessions designed to work on and improve balance.

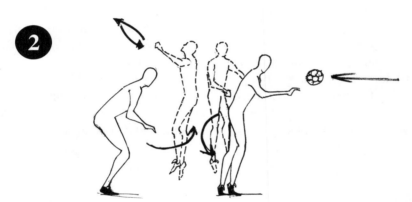

Purpose:

Improve the sense of balance and acrobatic skills.

Procedure:

The goalkeeper performs a forward somersault before saving the shot that the coach takes from a distance of about 10 yds.

Variation:

The keeper can perform a diving somersault over a hurdle.

Number of repetitions:

4-6 before suitable recovery.

Notes:

Performing this exercise the goalkeeper learns to recover his balance and the sense of position after losing them in the somersault.

Especially suggested for:

All goalkeepers in training sessions designed to work on and enhance balance and acrobatic skills.

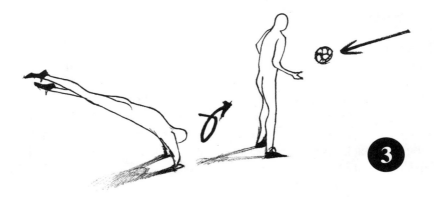

Drill n.4

Purpose:

Improve the sense of balance and acrobatic skills.

Procedure:

The goalkeeper performs a backward somersault before saving the shot that the coach takes from a distance of about 10 yds.

Number of repetitions:

4-6 before suitable recovery.

Notes:

Performing this exercise the goalkeeper learns to recover his balance and the sense of position after losing them in the somersault.

Especially suggested for:

All goalkeepers in training sessions designed to work on and enhance balance and acrobatic skills.

Drill n.5

Purpose:
Improve the sense of balance and acrobatic skills.

Procedure:
The goalkeeper performs a forward somersault that begins on one side outside of the goal mouth and ends inside it between the posts before saving the shot that the coach takes from the edge of the penalty box.

Number of repetitions:
4-6 before suitable recovery.

Notes:
Performing this exercise the goalkeeper learns to recover his balance and the sense of position after losing them in the somersault.

Especially suggested for:
All goalkeepers in training sessions designed to work on and enhance balance and acrobatic skills.

Drill n.6

Purpose:
Improve the sense of balance and acrobatic skills.

Procedure:
The goalkeeper performs a cartwheel that starts on one side of the goal and ends inside it; after making this acrobatic move, the keeper will stand facing the coach who shoots at goal from the edge of the penalty box.

Variation:
the goalkeeper concludes the cartwheel with his back to the coach and immediately turns to save the shot.

Number of repetitions:
4-6 before suitable recovery.

Notes:
Performing this exercise the goal-keeper learns to recover his balance and the sense of position after losing them in the cartwheel.

Especially suggested for:
All goalkeepers in training sessions designed to work on and enhance balance and acrobatic skills.

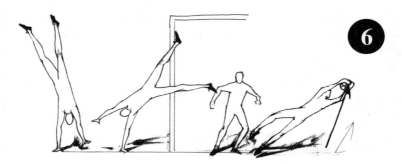

Drill n.7

Purpose:
Improve the sense of balance.

Procedure:
The goalkeeper spins rapidly for about 3-4 seconds until the coach gives the signal; at this point, the keeper stops to catch the shot that the coach takes from the edge of the penalty box.

Number of repetitions:
4-6 before suitable recovery.

Notes:
Performing this exercise the goal-keeper learns to recover his balance and the sense of position after losing them in the spin.

Especially suggested for:
All goalkeepers in training sessions designed to work on and enhance balance.

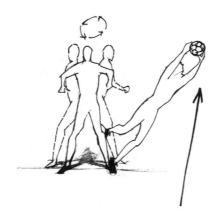

Drill n.8

Purpose:
Improve the sense of balance.

Procedure:
Two goalkeepers (n.1 and n.2) make a sort of round dance hand in hand in a 2 ye square area near one of the two posts; when the coach gives the signal (shouting "One!" for example), the keeper he calls moves into the goal and tries to catch the coach's shot.

Number of repetitions:
2-3 before suitable recovery.

Notes:
Performing this exercise the goalkeeper learns to recover his balance and the sense of position after losing them while turning round and round with his teammate.

Especially suggested for:
All goalkeepers in training sessions designed to work on and improve balance and acrobatic skills.

Drill n.9

Purpose:
Improve the sense of balance and acrobatic skills.

Procedure:
The goalkeeper jumps over a teammate like on a vaulting horse and immediately tries to catch the coach's shot when he lands on the ground.

Number of repetitions:
4-6 before suitable recovery.

Notes:
Performing this exercise the goalkeeper learns to recover his balance and the sense of position after losing them when jumping over his teammate.

Especially suggested for:
All goalkeepers in training sessions designed to work on and enhance balance and acrobatic skills.

Drill n.10

Purpose:
Improve the sense of balance and acrobatic skills.

Procedure:
The goalkeeper does a handstand with the support of one of his teammates who holds his ankles; when the coach gives the signal, the assistant teammate releases the ankles and the keeper immediately moves into the best position to try to catch the coach's shot.

Number of repetitions:
3-4 before suitable recovery.

Notes:
Performing this exercise the goalkeeper learns to recover his balance and the sense of position after losing them in the handstand.

Especially suggested for:
All goalkeepers in training sessions designed to work on and enhance balance and acrobatic skills.

9.1 Theoretical model

This statement may sound rather original, but we can clearly say that the goalkeeper is not a soccer player.

In fact, the goalkeeper differs from his field teammates not only for his physical, technical and physiological attributes, but also because he is the only one who mostly plays using his hands.

Goalkeeper's height

In the past, the average height of soccer goalkeepers in Italy was about 5'9", both because the average height of Italian people hardly reached 5'7" and because it was generally thought that tall athletes could hardly make the quick and rapid moves that the goalkeeper's position requires. However, thanks to the development of new training methods and the general increase in people's average height, the parameter for soccer goalkeepers has increased to about 6'1".

We do not mean to discourage those who are not very tall - in the past, goalkeepers of modest height also achieved great success - the most important thing, in fact, is to be aware of one's means and be able to use one's technical and physical qualities to make up for one's weaknesses.

Goalkeeper's profile

Soccer goalkeepers must have many special qualities; first of all, they must be agile in their movements, have quick reflexes, be able to keep their balance and "master" the ball; furthermore, they must also have a good dose of courage, strong legs (explosive and reactive), an excellent tactical sense (ability to read the situations), a strong personality and marked decision-making power.

In short, the goalkeeper must be a complete athlete.

9.2 Physical attributes

If you analyze the goalkeeper's performance carefully, you can notice that he runs much less than his field teammates; consequently, this means that there are many and clear differences from the physiological point of view, that his moves have a very short duration and are performed in small spaces, that his physical and athletic qualities are usually different from those of the other members of the team.

Considering all these important differences, you can clearly understand that it is also fundamental to differentiate coaching and training methods and work out special programs for goalkeepers.

Nevertheless, goalkeepers generally practiced with all their teammates until some years ago and only a very short period of time at the end of the training session was dedicated to them, at most. Obviously, specific training generally proved to be even more exhausting and physically demanding for the keeper in those conditions because it combined with the work loads that he had previously had with the whole team.

Training methods - as far as the athletic aspect in particular is concerned - were also the same: this means that goalkeepers were usually trained like midfield players, who generally run about 6 to 7.5 miles a match on average!

As far as strength is concerned, the training methods used for soccer goalkeepers were those typical of an endurance strength performance; in the end, the keeper was also trained hard from the point of view of lactic acid production.

However, things have improved in the last few years, thanks to the specialization of two important figures in soccer: the goalkeeper coach and the fitness coach.

The goalkeeper's physiological model is well known today; from the point of view of energy demand, the goalkeeper's performance can be considered as an alactacid anaerobic-type performance and not a lactacid anaerobic-type activity as is the case with his field teammates.

Therefore, practice sessions should only aim at improving the specific physical qualities that can help enhance their performance.

9.3 Useful fitness conditioning methods for goalkeepers

Special training for aerobic components

The most evident difference between the goalkeeper and his outfield teammates is the distance they cover running. Field players generally run 5 to 8 miles during the course of a standard match, depending on their positions; by contrast, the keeper does not run, he simply makes short sprints at most with long rest intervals in between. This means that goalkeepers' fitness needs differ greatly from those of his teammates and that special training to improve endurance qualities is not so useful for them; therefore, it is a real mistake to have the keeper perform every week all those aerobic activities that are usually suggested to the team (including long- or short-distance running, fartlek, jogging including changes of pace and so on).

However, increasing the goalkeeper's anaerobic threshold is an aspect that cannot be neglected completely; in fact, minimum conditioning practice to achieve this purpose can also help the keeper to reach a good and healthy physical condition in general and to improve his capacity to recover when exercising in training sessions that are often more intense and physically demanding than official competitions (consider, for instance, playing practice games in small-sized fields, or playing particular tactical situations, or repetitive shooting, and so on).

Specific training to improve the keeper's aerobic capacities should mainly be included in the pre-season conditioning phase in order to "build" a good general physical condition, but should also be recalled every month.

The training methods that we suggest to you to achieve this goal include: fartlek with short variations (up to 30 seconds at most), continuous running with a mixture of paces, or interval training on distances no longer than 150 to 200 yards in the pre-season conditioning period; continuous running with a mixture of paces or "intermittent" exercise by G. Cometti especially adjusted to goalkeepers to be performed once a month during the agonistic period.

"The organic technical circuit for goalkeepers" shown in diagram 1 is an interesting solution for "mixed" exercise, combining the most typical technical moves that are particularly favorable to train both aerobic and lactacid components.

9.4   Special training to improve muscle strength

We have always asserted that the goalkeeper must be a complete and all-around athlete; a well-proportioned body with strong and suitably developed muscles are required attributes for soccer goalkeepers.

Therefore, a complete conditioning program for goalkeepers should also include constant exercise to maintain and/or develop arm and torso muscles.

This type of exercise (excluding the legs) should be performed once a week at least by professional athletes and no less than once a month by amateur players; obviously, the work load must be combined with specific training (both technical practice on the field and fitness conditioning) supervised by the goalkeeper coach. The exercises to strengthen abdominal, dorsal and shoulder muscles can be performed at the end of the regular practice session or on those days when the coaching program does not include team practice.

An example of general muscle development to be performed in a gymnasium can include:

Pectorals on the bench: 2 sets of 10 repetitions each using weights at 60 to 70% of your maximum load (max);

Abdominals: 30 repetitions;

Dorsals: 2 sets of 10 repetitions each using weights at 60 to 70% of your max load;

Abdominals: 30 repetitions;

Deltoids: 2 sets of 10 repetition each using 4 to 6 kg dumb-bells;

Abdominals: 30 repetitions;

Brachial biceps: 2 sets of 10 repetitions each using a 30 to 40 kg bar;

Abdominals: 30 repetitions;

Torso rotation: 20 repetitions carrying a 10 kg bar on your shoulders.

A separate chapter is dedicated to strengthening the goalkeeper's leg muscles.

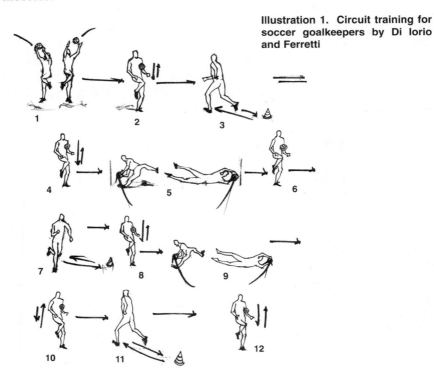

Illustration 1. Circuit training for soccer goalkeepers by Di Iorio and Ferretti

1. The goalkeeper performs 4 consecutive high saves taking off with the leg corresponding to the direction of the ball

2. 20 seconds juggling the ball with the feet (active recovery)

3. 50 yards running back and forth (shuttle run 25 + 25) at good intensity

4. 30 seconds juggling the ball with the feet (active recovery)

5. The goalkeeper performs 4 consecutive diving saves to catch ground shots

6. 20 seconds juggling the ball with the feet (active recovery)

7. 50 yards running back and forth (shuttle run 25 + 25) at a lower intensity than the previous one

8. 30 seconds juggling the ball with the feet (active recovery)

9. The goalkeeper performs 4 consecutive diving saves to catch mid-height shots

10. 20 seconds juggling the ball with the feet (active recovery)

11. 50 yards running back and forth (shuttle run 25 + 25) at good intensity

12. 30 seconds juggling the ball with the feet (active recovery)

13. 5-minute recovery interval at least before repeating the training circuit or before shifting to another activity

Notes: This training circuit can prove to be rather exhausting since the technical moves (apparently easy to perform) are introduced between athletic workouts (shuttle run) that cause both local (leg muscles) and general fatigue. From the psychological point of view, in fact, constantly repeating the various workouts with active recovery intervals not only enhances endurance aerobic components, but also brings about little lactic acid oxygen debt that the keeper especially perceives in the muscles that are mainly involved in the activity (lower limbs muscles).

Consequently, the coach must be able to adjust the recovery period between the stations (either increasing or decreasing the number of seconds allowed for active rest), the number of technical moves to perform (from four to two, from four to six, for example), the intensity of the run and, obviously, the number of times the training circuit should be repeated depending on the goalkeeper's conditioning level.

If you analyze the moves that a goalkeeper makes during the course of a match you can notice that his actions are generally short and rapid: he mainly makes explosive-type movements. This means that exercise should aim at improving speed and explosive strength, that is the ability that goalkeepers need to move rapidly towards the ball, to jump upward or dive in mid-air or on the ground. It is not important for soccer goal-keepers to train strength in their legs to develop muscle mass (maximal strength) or to perform consecutive leaps (endurance strength), but it is fundamental for them to train their capacity to apply the right amount of strength to make the technical move (the save) in an explosive and rapid manner and in the shortest time possible.

Making the goalkeeper train endurance strength or maximal strength as frequently as his teammates is a mistake; consequently, a specific strength training program especially designed for soccer goalkeepers must only be focused on enhancing speed and explosive strength.

Therefore, from the practical point of view it would be advisable to avoid prolonged sets of leaps (for instance, 4 sets of 8 to 10 repetitions) but also endurance strength circuit training on isotonic machines (for example, sets of 10 repetitions using weights at 60% of your maximal load on the press or on the leg extension machine).

9.5 Special training to improve lactacid anaerobic capacities

It is common knowledge that training the lactacid anaerobic mechanism is important for soccer players; this energy mechanism is not so important for the goalkeeper, by contrast; this means that also from this point of view the keeper cannot be considered a standard soccer player.

In reality, soccer goalkeepers never apply to their lactic acid anaerobic energy mechanism during the course of a match; in fact, their actions and moves are very rapid, last a very few seconds and are hardly performed consecutively. Therefore, the energy process they "use" most is the alactacid anaerobic mechanism. Moreover, the long rest intervals between actions also prevent the onset of lactic acid oxygen debt resulting from continuous storage (which means several alactacid-type actions with short intervals in between).

In short, it is practically useless for the keeper to practice lactic acid-type training together with the rest of the team and it is definitely better for him to "invest" his time in training the technical, physical and athletic qualities that specifically characterize his position.

However, lactic acid-type exercise should not be excluded from weekly training programs completely; in some particular team conditioning sessions (including shooting at goal, strenuous tactical practice, conditioned games in small-sized fields, for example) the activity is so intense and repetitive that it is almost impossible to prevent the onset of lactic acid oxygen debt. Anyway, those extreme situations do not occur in regular official competitions; this is why training the lactic acid anaerobic mechanism should not become a priority in the goalkeeper's physical conditioning program.

Goalkeepers are not allowed to make mistakes since every error they make pays a high price. In fact, if the keeper fails to do something, there are no possibilities for him and his team to make up for his error; furthermore, the mistakes that goalkeepers make are evident to everybody and this can cause dramatic psychological consequences. If the keeper lets in a goal, there is always somebody who is ready to point out the fact that the keeper could have saved that ball; moreover, if he makes a gross error, great perplexity immediately arises about the possibility to rely on him in the future, even if he was a real "hero" in the previous match.

Goalkeepers have little to justify themselves; this is why it is important to help them - especially youth keepers - understand that mistakes are always just round the corner and if they do not have a strong personality, they can hardly overcome negative and unsuccessful events and become top-class keepers.

Good goalkeepers are not those who never make an error, but those who make fewer mistakes than the others.

From the point of view of individual personality it is possible to find exuberant, extroverted and excessively bold goalkeepers who like acting as protagonists through their hyperactive attitude; their behavior during the competition is even too easy since they need to attest their leadership through authoritarian acts (their voice is the guide of their team's defensive actions); their diving saves are often acrobatic moves and tend to stress the spectacular nature of their movements.

On the other hand, you can also find goalkeepers having opposed characteristics from the psychological point of view; reflective athletes, tending to think and reason, little inclined to spectacular actions and prone to essential moves. Their presence inside the group is generally discreet; yet their performance is worthy of notice. A good coach should be able to adjust his coaching method and program to the personality of his goalkeepers, trying to exploit and exalt their own physical and psychological qualities.

Emotions and the way they can affect the performance are another important aspect for soccer goalkeepers. It may happen that excellent keepers limit and condition their behaviors because they are seized by strong emotions, they do not take the initiative because they are afraid of making mistakes, they simply avoid running risks and live actions and events as unarmed spectators; moreover, when they get involved in the action they try to reduce the length of their moves without carefully considering the inner dynamic of the action itself. Goalkeepers with this kind of personality generally find it difficult to take decisions, take full responsibilities for anything and are always reluctant to come off the line. They always feel the need to prove to themselves that they are up to their tasks, and only when they can make a successful save on the first shot are they convinced that it is their lucky day. One of the coach's duties is to help his players understand that a good goalkeeper is required to play in the best way possible in relation to his technical, tactical and physical characteristics; actually, psychological implications are not considered to be good reasons to justify a poor performance and are only tolerated in the youth period.

The favorable position as the last defender allows the keeper to monitor and assess the opponents' movements better than his teammates can; this situation allows him to suggest to his defending teammates the best countermeasures to take to build a successful defensive action. Consequently, every suggestion the goalkeeper gives must be accepted and carried out in practice. For this to be possible, the keeper must be accepted as a "leader" by his teammates. Everything he tells them must be well aimed and justified; useless exaggerations would create a very bad relation with the team, thus "invalidating" the benefit of his suggestions. For example, there are situations where the goalkeeper calls for a back pass while his defending teammate ventures on dangerous dribbles - maybe because he wants to exhibit his skills, in some cases - running the risk of losing possession of the ball and putting the whole team, and the goalkeeper in particular, in a seriously difficult situation. In those cases, the keeper must be firm and resolute at calling for the ball; on the other hand, if his teammates hardly give back passes to him, the coach must intervene to set the right behavior inside the team; in fact, all the players should trust their keeper and they should also know that he bears full responsibility for the decisions he takes.

Also when the goalkeeper comes off the line and firmly calls for the ball to make a high save, all his outfield teammates must act and move accordingly so as to favor the keeper's action; those who are standing along the ball trajectory should try to avoid touching the ball so as to help the goalkeeper's high save, while those who are standing near the goal should replace the keeper on the line. When the goalkeeper decides to make a high or a low save, he must be firm and resolute in his movements, calling for the ball before one of his teammates gets to it; hesitation and indecision, in fact, can result in unfavorable deflections of the ball and/or can cause the classic own goal to be scored. As a general rule, in order to "train" the goalkeeper's character it is advisable to encourage him to run the risk of trying an unsuccessful save rather than stop midway between the ball and the goal. This does not mean that the keeper should be encouraged to act rashly without considering the situation carefully, but that he should be stimulated to take his own responsibilities.

The goalkeeper should feel he is an integral part of the whole defensive line and move in relation to them; actually, the keeper is not the only player who can prevent a goal from being scored, since it is possible to check the opposition's offensive build-up through the cooperation and the combined actions of the whole defending line. How many times has the goalkeeper saved a dangerous situation resulting from an unsuccessful offside, acting as a "sweeper" in the defending line, and how many times is the keeper required to take an active part in starting the offensive build-up?

You can also see goalkeepers who often make the serious mistake of reproaching one of their teammates openly on the field, embarrassing him directly in front of the spectators; in this way, the team spirit is inevitably undermined and the relations of mutual esteem and respect that should prevail inside a group are broken down; this is not the right way for the goalkeeper to act as a leader.

Certainly, in the career of any goalkeeper - from those who play in first division to those in the minor amateur championships - there have been moments when everything seemed dramatically difficult and even the easiest move or save appeared to be an obstacle to them; in those cases, it may happen that discouragement combined with a resigned and mistrustful attitude towards your skills inevitably get control over your state of mind, negatively influencing your conviction that you can become an excellent goalkeeper.

Morphological and technical features being equal, having a strong or a weak will to achieve the final goal definitely helps select many athletes. A player will never reach the top level if he does not have a strong will to reach a goal or to assert and strengthen his own "ego" or if he does not develop a more critical attitude that can help him understand his responsibilities completely.

11.1   Pre-season coaching plan for youth goalkeepers

What we are going to suggest in the following pages is not a program that the coach can introduce at the odd moments during the course of the standard training session, but a different way to consider the youth goalkeeper's position so that he is no longer "excluded" from the others in the practice sessions; on the contrary, the youth keeper is encouraged and motivated in his personal growth process by using a new model for a harmonic and progressive development.

The traditional coaching methods used in many youth systems - that are not based on careful planning, very often - should be definitely abandoned and replaced by suitable coaching methods based on the direct knowledge and development of all the various coordination capacities.

The most important ones include: space-and-time orientation, anticipation, reaction, differentiation and combination skills, hand-eye coordination.

It is useful to remember that in the 10-to-14-year-old age group the coaching program cannot primarily aim at enhancing physical and athletic capacities, since those features will improve as coordination capacities gradually improve and become more refined. In this regard, we would suggest to film all the technical moves that youth goalkeepers make the very first days of their pre-season conditioning camp in order to analyze them with the player directly and correct possible mistakes. In this way, it is also possible to plan the following training sessions on the errors and weaknesses that the keeper has shown in the videos.

Anticipation skill

Anticipation skill is an important quality that allows the goalkeeper to understand the opposition's and his teammates' plans of action, thus favoring his own motor task.

How can anticipation skill be trained and improved?

In the starting phase it is fundamental that the goalkeeper masters basic soccer technique more or less in the same way his teammates do. For this reason, he must know the difference between an instep kick and a pass or shot made with the inner or the outer instep. In this regard, we generally suggest to plan some coaching sessions focusing on basic general technique, not only because most of the goalkeeper's moves are made using the feet, but also because in this way he can better understand and assess the shots that the opposition take at his goal. Certainly, it is not easy for the keeper to "coordinate" his movements with all the other systems interacting with him (the ball, his body position, his teammates, the opponents, the distance and so forth), but this capacity is really very helpful both to read the situation and choose and perform the best saving action.

Among all the possible training methods we suggest various exercises involving the goalkeeper to bounce the ball on the ground or against a wall while walking and running also moving sideways and backward; throw the ball against the goal posts and the crossbar so as to "feel" the goal and its size; throw the ball in pairs using standard balls and balls of different colors, weights and shapes so as to gradually introduce the perception and mental representation of the various ball trajectories. In this starting phase of planned work it is also important to introduce the first exercises on fine / refined agility that are necessary to learn, internalize and rapidly master any new body movement and adjust it to the different situations of play. It is fundamental to remember that achieving a high level of agility considerably helps enhance quick reflexes, recover lost balance, improve catching skills, acrobatic abilities and individual courage as well.

We suggest you train agility qualities in every conditioning session, increasing the level of difficulty progressively until you have the goalkeeper conclude the exercise with a final save (complex agility skills). See diagrams no. 1, 2, 3 and 4.

The main "variations" of the exercises suggested principally aim at improving agility skills combined with a proper diving technique, overcoming the discomfort and the difficulties that the goalkeeper faces as a result of abandoning the ball in his possession. In this way, mental attention is considerably stimulated and enhanced.

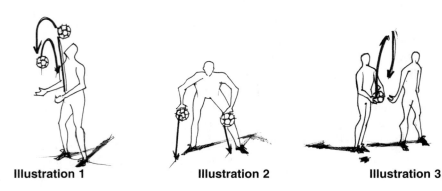

Illustration 1   **Illustration 2**   **Illustration 3**

136

Illustration 4

Orientation skill

It is absolutely fundamental that the goalkeeper can "feel the goal" in relation to the position of the ball and is able to anticipate the movements that the opposition are going to make and carefully assess how those moves can influence the development of his own action. In order to become the real master of the goal and the penalty box the athlete should be trained to perceive the events correctly, his peripheral vision and his capacity to analyze the development of play should be stimulated in order to favor suitable and proper positioning.

At the beginning it is advisable to train the young goalkeeper to take up the right position between the two posts following the rule according to which one should stand along the bisecting line of the useful shooting angle that the shooter has at his disposal; at the same time, starting at the age of 10, it is important to enhance the sensorial analyzers that are responsible for all the information the goalkeeper receives from the outside, especially the visual and the auditory ones.

The exercises shown in diagrams no. 5 and 6 increase the capacities of the visual analyzers and also improve agility and technique, which helps the youth keeper understand what is happening around him (ability to read the game). We advise you to introduce these activities in the warm-up phase every day.

In order to train the auditory analyzers you can ask the goalkeeper to position and stand blindfolded in the middle of the goal and move inside the goal using the information and the points of reference he perceived when he had his eyes open. Always standing blindfold, he must also be able to take up the best position in relation to the coach's call or the ball bouncing on the ground and also check the right position with the help of the coach. In this way, the goalkeeper is gradually trained to "feel the goal" and its fixed points of reference (the upright posts, the six-yard and the penalty boxes, the penalty spot).

If you want to work on space-and-time orientation skills, we suggest you an exercise (see illusration 7) whose main purpose is to gradually get to taking up the best position (the coach should always point out that it is definitely more difficult for the keeper to make a successful save if he is not standing in the right waiting position, but is moving to try to find the right posture). It is advisable to develop this kind of training especially in the first ten days of the pre-season conditioning period, in the phase immediately following the warm-up.

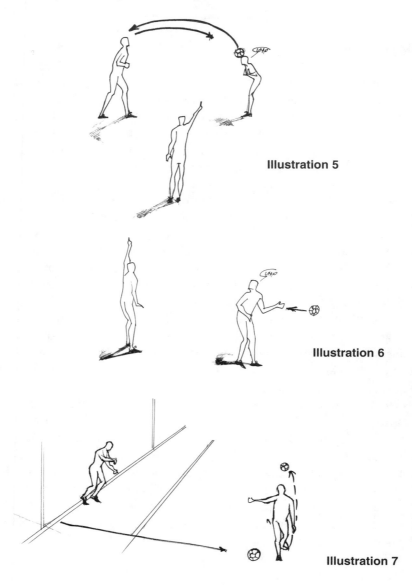

Illustration 5

Illustration 6

Illustration 7

Differentiation and combination skills

The differentiation capacity allows the goalkeeper to "modulate" upward push carefully and control the contraction of his hand muscles to stop or deflect a ball.

Is it possible to make youth goalkeepers understand the importance of developing this skill?

We generally suggest you use the method of drastically pointing out the negative effects of any mistake, focusing the attention on the technique of the bad move to finally make the keeper perform it in a proper and natural manner. Here is a useful example that can help make this concept clearer to understand: force the goalkeeper to keep his arms and hands rigid to catch shots coming straight at his chest, then ask him to perform the technical move correctly pointing out the contrast. Or you can also ask the keeper to keep his hand unlocked to punch the ball away high in the air and then make him deflect the ball in a much more natural manner.

Obviously, you can use this method to train the keeper to handle the basic technical principles of his position: the standard waiting position, catching, diving, punching technique and so on... For example, if a keeper is standing in the basic ready position keeping his legs too wide apart, he will have to perform the exercise keeping his legs excessively wide apart, so that he can understand that he is making a mistake which inevitably delays the saving action. The same technique should be used for a goalkeeper standing with his legs too close together (remember that the distance between the two legs should correspond to the distance between the two shoulders, more or less).

In the same training phase, in addition to coaching the basic technical moves characterizing the goalkeeper's position, it is also necessary to train the player to coordinate the partial movements of his body in relation to the final movement he make to execute the save. For instance: making a ground diving save involves the keeper driving the inside leg compared to the ball direction sideways and forward, lowering the trunk and stretching out his hands forward to catch the ball. As you can understand, there are various motor phases that must be combined together to result in a successful action. With regard to the saving technique we have taken into consideration above, we suggest a training program including exercises that you already know but that are truly effective and successful to achieve the purpose. See illustrations no. 8, 9 and 10.

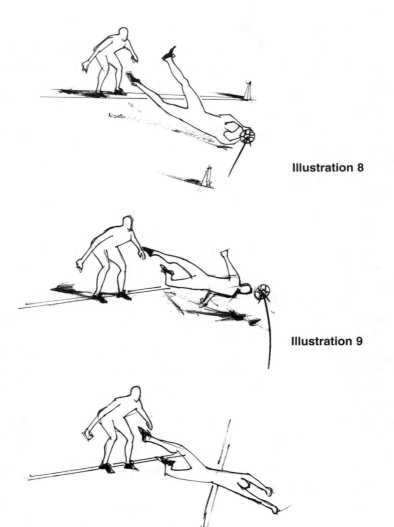

Illustration 8

Illustration 9

Illustration 10

Reaction skill

This skill allows the goalkeeper to respond to external stimuli rapidly and make suitable movements. Intuition - which means the instant perception of how the opponent's action is developing - considerably favors reaction speed. Quick reaction skills find their practical application in the speed of motion that allows the goalkeeper to perform all the various moves that his position requires.

In addition to running and moving sideways, in fact, soccer goalkeepers are required to develop complex and specific dynamics of motion so that they can always master the situation on any occasion. The main process to train quick reflexes and reactions is based on the perfect performance - that must become absolutely automatic - of the various technical moves combined with the dynamic force and the constant repetition of the same exercises at high speed and rhythm. Then, the youth goalkeeper will have to work on basic leg coordination, making skips forward and sideways, running while raising his heels up to his buttocks, making slaloms around posts so as to help enhance coordination between lower and upper limbs. Later on, after some 4 or 5 days of pre-season training, it is possible to introduce the first exercises and activities to practice the skill in question (see diagrams no. 11, 12 and 13).

Moreover, in the summer pre-season conditioning period we also suggest you attach some importance to the starting pre-acrobatic activities to train balance. The exercises that we show you are characterized by a growing level of difficulty and must all end with a final dive to try to intercept the coach's shot (this is to differentiate the workouts in relation to the goalkeeper's specific position and to make the exercises more enjoyable to perform). Introduce two or three exercises every day to finally perform the whole sequence after 10 days of preliminary practice.

1. The goalkeeper is standing with his back to the coach and immediately turns about to catch his shot when the coach gives the signal.

2. The goalkeeper is standing facing the coach; he turns 360° and tries to intercept the coach's shot.

3. The goalkeeper performs a somersault forward and immediately positions to save the coach's shot.

4. The goalkeeper performs a somersault backward and immediately positions to catch the coach's shot.

5. The goalkeeper performs a cartwheel on the side of the goal, outside the goal mouth, and rapidly positions to save the coach's shot.

6. The goalkeeper performs a somersault with the support of one of his teammates. The teammate assists and helps the keeper to complete the

somersault. At the end of the acrobatic movement the goalkeeper tries to intercept the coach's shot.

7. Two goalkeepers move around themselves almost as if they were standing on the spot, pulling each other out of the goal by their hands; when the coach calls one of them, that goalkeeper promptly moves to position inside the goal to try to save the coach's shot.

8. The goalkeeper is standing in the middle of the goal and rapidly spins around for about 5 to 6 seconds; when the coach gives the starting signal, he immediately takes up the right position to intercept the coach's shot.

9. The goalkeeper vaults leaping over his teammate's back and immediately positions to try to catch the coach's shot.

10. Starting from a handstand position, balancing on his hands (also with the help of one of his teammates), the goalkeeper lets himself fall down and positions to save the coach's shot.

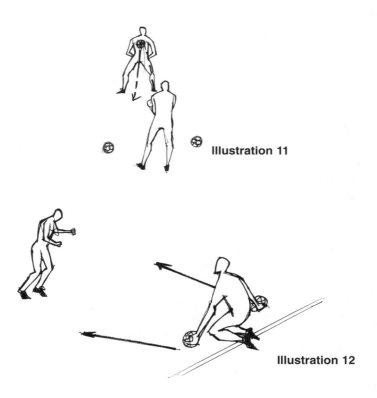

Illustration 11

Illustration 12

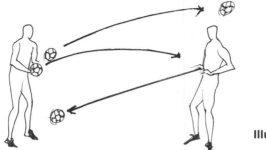

Illustration 13

High ball trajectories

A good goalkeeper should always play an active role in facing the opposition's attacking action, always trying to anticipate the collective development of their maneuver. This is especially important in the case of balls coming straight or from the flanks of the field and describing high paths. A goalkeeper that takes off in the middle of the penalty box to catch a high shot or cross not only breaks the attacking action that the opponents are building, but also prevents the ball from being deflected or cleared back by his defending teammates.

How is it possible to train youth keepers to anticipate the ball trajectory and understand whether they can get to it successfully?

The situations that we show you in the next page aim at activating the mental processes that can help read and anticipate the path of the ball and also emphasize whether the exercise has been performed successfully or not. These exercises stimulate mental processing that allows the keeper to understand the exact time and place the ball will land and also help practice high saving technique (see diagrams no. 14, 15 and 16).

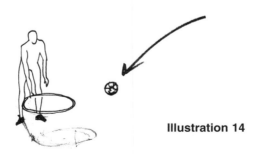

Illustration 14

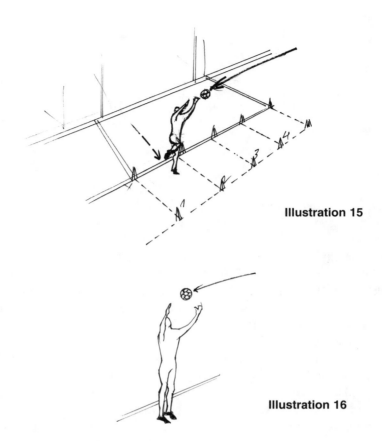

Illustration 15

Illustration 16

11.2 EXERCISES
In the pre-season conditioning period

Exercise no.1

Stand upright holding two balls,
one in each hand, throw them upward
simultaneously and catch them using
the hand opposite to the one that first
threw the ball.
Variation:
When the coach gives the signal, throw
the balls upward and promptly catch the
coach's shot.

Exercise no.2

Bounce two balls on the ground
simultaneously, using both hands.
Variation:
When the coach gives the signal, throw
the balls upward and promptly catch the
coach's shot.

Exercise no.3

Hold the ball at the height of your stomach,
throw it upward and catch it behind your
back.
Variation:
After catching the ball, promptly position
to intercept the coach's shot.

Exercise no.4

Start with your arms stretched out forward,
holding the ball; then, release your hold
to clap your hand and catch the ball again
before it falls.

Variation:
After catching the ball, promptly position
to intercept the coach's shot.

Exercise no.5

Two goalkeepers are standing about 5
to 6 yards apart heading the ball to
each other; at the same time they also
keep their eyes on the coach's hands
to shout the number he is showing with
his fingers.

Exercise no.6

The goalkeeper positions in front of
three fellow keepers who are standing
at a distance of about 10 yards one from
another. If goalkeeper A raises his arm,
D passes the ball to C, if
C raises his arm D passes to A. If both
C and A raise their arms, the ball is
played to B; the same thing happens if
C and A do not raise their arms.

Exercise no.7

Before trying to catch the coach's shot,
the goalkeeper turns his head to see
and repeats loud the number that one of
his teammates is showing him with his
hands.

Exercise no.8

Starting from the goal line the goalkeeper
calmly positions on one of the two balls
that the coach suggests to him and tries to
intercept the shot. Immediately afterwards
he performs the same exercise speeding up

the movements he makes to take up the right
position, avoiding handling the shot while
he is still moving, with the trunk too high,
his legs wide apart and not parallel. After
giving the starting signal the coach rapidly
takes the shot. The coach must help the
goalkeeper understand the different
possibilities he has to make a successful save
in one situation and the other.

Exercise no.9

Force the goalkeeper to dive sideways
and forward inside the area marked by
the cones and combine the various phases.

Exercise no.10

Starting from the goal line on one side of
the goal, head the ball while diving before
it touches the ground to make the keeper
understand the importance of diving
sideways and forward.

Exercise no.11

Starting from the goal line, combine all
the various phases of the saving action;
you are obliged to pass under a rope about
2 to 2.5 feet high.

Exercise no.12

The goalkeeper is standing behind his coach
who is holding a ball called ball no.3 and
is standing between two balls called ball
no. 1 and ball no.2. The coach throws the
ball no.3 against the goalkeeper's back
and immediately calls the number of the
ball that keeper has to catch.

Exercise no.13

The coach is resting on his knees with two
balls placed on the ground, called even and
uneven ball, at a distance of about 4 to 5
yards from the goalkeeper. The coach
throws both balls and when they are midway
between himself and the goalkeeper, he
shouts a number (an even or uneven number)
and the goalkeeper promptly positions to
intercept the ball the coach has called.

Exercise no.14

The goalkeeper is holding two balls in his
hands that he throws to the coach standing
at a distance of about 5 to 6 yards. Only
one of the two balls is played back to
the keeper, who has to position quickly
to try to catch it.

Exercise no.15

The coach throws the ball to the goalkeeper
so as to make it describe a high path; before
the ball begins its way down, the keeper -
who is standing at a distance of about 20
yards form the coach - places a hoop on the
ground to show the spot where the ball will
land.
Alternate the exercise trying to intercept
the ball immediately after it bounces on the
ground, keeping your hands stretched out
forward. This seemingly simple exercise lays bare all the
difficulties that a young goalkeeper has
in processing the exact time and place
where the ball will land.

Exercise no.16

The goalkeeper positions in the middle of
his goal. The coach marks out 4 square areas
about 3 to 4 yards wide near the edge of
the goal box; then, he takes a lobbed shot
from the flanks of the field.
When the ball begins its downward path, the
keeper immediately shouts the number
of the square where he will move to
intercept the ball with a high save.
Variation:
Perform the same exercise trying to
intercept high balls coming straight from
in front.

Exercise no.17

The coach crosses the ball from the
flanks of the field and the goalkeeper
must immediately understand the exact
time and place where the ball will land,
moving to stand below the ball in the
standard waiting position (standing
totally motionless and with his arms
stretched out upward) to catch it.
After positioning on the right landing
spot, the goalkeeper must stand
motionless raising his arms upward
and check whether his reading of the ball
trajectory has been successful or not.

11.3   The standard training week of a soccer goalkeeper

A weekly conditioning program for soccer goalkeepers, the work
being divided in three different sessions. The program we are going to
suggest includes a wide range of exercises and activities.
When a coach plans the standard training week he must necessarily
set some goals that tend to enhance or maintain the goalkeeper's general

performance and condition; in particular, a successful conditioning program should:

- stimulate and develop all the technical principles peculiar to this position;
- enhance anticipation skills;
- help and favor quick reactions.

It is also fundamental for a coach to take into proper account the means that he has at his disposal for training and do everything he can to get the minimum equipment he needs.

In the training program we suggest in the following pages you will need: two poles to form a goal, some balls, three or four tennis balls, some flat cones to mark out some square areas and a hurdle whose height can be changed.

If you do not have a fellow coach working with the goalkeepers - as is usually the case in most amateur clubs - we advise you to start coaching the goalkeepers about 35 to 40 minutes before the regular training session for the whole team.

Having the goalkeepers practice together with the rest of the team should be a priority for the coach, but don't forget that the specific qualities peculiar to the keeper's position can only be improved through specific training.

In particular, we refer to:

- agility
- balance
- acrobatic skills
- the sense of positioning
- saving skills (high and ground saves) combined with the ability to read ball trajectories
- courage
- and so on............

If these qualities are suitably trained, they can be enhanced, or maintained at least, through well-aimed conditioning planning.

Here are some suggestions for you:

For those who did not play as goalkeepers in the past it could be difficult to advise the keeper on some particular technical, tactical and psychological behaviors to adopt without running the risk of being approximate and inaccurate. I believe that it is helpful to remind your goalkeepers of a few things unequivocally.

On the balls coming straight from in front and describing high paths: jump upward and forward.

150

On the balls coming from the flanks of the field and describing high paths: always focus your attention on the take-off leg which must be the right leg for the balls coming from your right side and the left one to handle the balls coming from the left (a different way and position to prepare the high save would delay the saving action).

When making diving saves: always point out that the correct technique involves the goalkeeper taking a step sideways and forward with the inside leg compared to the direction of the ball; in this way he moves towards the ball.

When handling close-in shots: tell your goalkeepers to stand motionless as long as possible in order to avoid favoring the opponent. They should try to avoid "sitting down" on the ground and make the dive fully extended forward.

TUESDAY

Warm-up
  4 minutes stretching;
  10 minutes warm-up using the ball.
  1. Three or four goalkeepers dribble the ball inside a 20-yard wide square area. When the coach gives the starting signal, each keeper wins possession of the ball of one of his teammates, taking care not to remain in possession of his own ball. Duration of the exercise: 2 minutes.
  2. The goalkeepers juggle the ball with their feet; when the coach gives the starting signal, they all kick the ball in the air and promptly take off high forward to catch it with their hands. Duration: 2 minutes.
  3. Three or four goalkeepers rapidly pass the ball to each other without stopping running inside a 10-yard wide square area. At the beginning they make passes using their hands, then they take volley kicks, then they make the ball pass below their thighs, finally they make heading volleys and passes like in basketball. Each conditioned move lasts about 40 to 50 seconds for an overall duration of about 4 to 5 minutes.
  N.B.: 1 or 2 minutes stretching at the end.

Exercises to develop visual analyzers (duration: 6 minutes)
  1. The goalkeeper positions to face three players at a distance of about 10 yards. If player A raises his arm, D (the goalkeeper who is practicing) passes the ball to C and if C raises his arm D passes to A. If C and A both raise one of their arms or do not raise them, D passes the ball to

B. Perform the exercise without stopping for about 60 to 80 seconds.

2. The goalkeeper B positions in line between two teammates at a distance of about 15 to 20 yards from each one of them and stands facing the player in possession of the ball. When the ball is passed to him, the keeper turns towards the other teammate and plays the ball to him if he does not have his arm raised; otherwise, he passes the ball back to the player who played the ball to him.

Exercises to practice catching skills and to feel the contact with the ground

Duration: 6 minutes.

1. The coach takes a hard shot just above the goalkeeper's face from a distance of about 6 to 7 yards. The keeper is sitting on the ground with his legs slightly bent.

2. The same as above, but in this case the goalkeeper lets his trunk fall down on one side and ends his catching action with the help of the ground.

3. The same as above, but with the sole variation that in this case the goalkeeper is resting on his knees.

Exercises to improve and maintain lower limbs muscle strength

1. Lay down on the ground face up; when the coach gives the starting signal, rapidly stand up and try to intercept a mid-height shot with a sideways diving save.

2. Lay down on the ground face down; quickly stand up and try to intercept a mid-height shot with a sideways diving save.

3. Lay on the ground face up; take your legs behind your head and make a quick leap to try to intercept a mid-height shot with a sideways diving save.

4. Start down on your knees; make a quick leap to recover the standard waiting position to try to intercept a mid-height shot with a sideways diving save.

5. Raise your knees up to your chest 2 to 4 times and then try to intercept a mid-height shot with a sideways diving save.

6. Lay down on the ground on one side; when the coach gives the starting signal, stand up quickly and try to intercept a mid-height shot with a sideways diving save.

7. Jump over a mid-height hurdle and try to catch a ball with a high save in the air.

8. Jump over a mid-height hurdle and try to intercept a ball with a high save in the air while passing over the hurdle.

9. Pass over a mid-height hurdle making a somersault forward and try to catch a ball with a high save in the air.

10. Pass over a hurdle and try to catch a ball with a high save in the air.

N.B.: Repeat each exercise 4 to 6 times.

WEDNESDAY - THURSDAY

Warm-up
Start the training session with 4 minutes of stretching and begin the warm-up phase.

1. Three goalkeepers form a triangle; at the vertex of the triangle is the practicing keeper; he makes sideways movements backward to intercept alternately the balls that one teammate and the other play to him. The ball is thrown so as to make it bounce on the ground and directed at the goalkeeper's chest and above his head.

2. Three goalkeepers form a triangle; at the vertex of the triangle is the practicing keeper; he makes sideways movements forward to intercept alternately the balls that one teammate and the other play to him. The ball is thrown so as to make it bounce on the ground and directed at the goalkeeper's chest and above his head.

N.B.: At the end make short jumps to improve coordination for about 4 minutes (different types of low hops to cover a distance of 7 to 8 yards and skips over a distance of 5 yards).

Exercises to improve quick reactions (plyometrics)
9 minutes of plyometric exercises with the ball (use a box about 1.5 to 2 feet high).

1. Jump down six times forward, six times on the right and six times on the left; after each jump the goalkeeper tries to catch the ball promptly leaping forward.

2. Jump down from the box (two times forward and two times sideways), jump over three high hurdles, skip and sprint over a distance of about 3 to 4 yards.

N.B.: perform some stretching between the sets. At the end perform some special exercises to release back muscles contraction.
Performance speed and reaction skills
Use two goals 6 yards wide placed at a distance of 12 to 15 yards from each other.

1. Two goalkeepers, each one holding a ball in his hands; when the

coach gives the starting signal, they throw the ball to each other and catch the ball of their teammate.

2. Two goalkeepers, each one holding a ball in his hands; when the coach gives the starting signal, they take a volley kick to each other and catch the ball of their teammate.

3. When the coach gives the starting signal, a goalkeeper moves towards his teammate's goal to shoot the ball placed in the middle on the ground, while the other keeper moves towards the opposite goal to try to intercept the shot taken by his teammate.

Correct and accurate performance technique
Duration: 12 minutes.

1. Start from the goal line and calmly move to position on the ball suggested by the coach and intercept the shot. The coach must correct any mistake resulting from bad positioning technique.

2. Start from the goal line and quickly move to position on the ball suggested by the coach and intercept the shot. The coach must correct any mistake resulting from bad positioning technique.

N.B.: This exercise helps make the goalkeeper understand that during the match he does not always have the time to position properly and that it is important, therefore, to take up the right position, keep dynamic balance and keep one's body under constant control.

3. The goalkeeper is standing at the near post; when the coach gives the starting signal, he promptly recovers his position to handle the ball that is passing over his head towards the far post. The coach waits for the keeper to take the right position and shoots at goal. Repeat the same exercise with the coach waiting a very short time before shooting.

Exercises to develop a different technique to prepare the saving move when the position of the ball varies
Duration: 10 minutes.

1. The goalkeeper is standing in a low position trying not to fall on the ground and faces the player in possession of the ball who is positioned slightly wide compared to the goal; the attacker passes the ball to his central teammate, the keeper promptly adjusts his position to commit the player receiving the ball and tries to intercept the ball with a ground save if his hypothetical opponent misses the control or stands motionless in the waiting position in case the opponent shoots at goal.

2. The ball is shot several times against the goalkeeper, who is standing at the near post; when the ball is played to the assistant coach stand-

ing just outside the goal box, the keeper immediately changes his position and tries to intercept the shot taken by the assistant coach.

N.B.: The exercises we have suggested must always comply with the needs of the whole team and can be introduced between team tactical activities. If you do not have enough time at your disposal, skip the plyometric workouts at the end of the training session.

FRIDAY

Warm-up
Start the training session with 4 minutes of stretching followed by general warm-up.

1. Four goalkeepers move around inside a square area (10 yards wide) throwing the ball to each other. The player in possession of the ball shouts the name of a third keeper to suggest to his teammate to whom he must throw the ball he has just received. Purpose: enhance attention and reasoning. Duration: 2 minutes.

2. Four to five goalkeepers form a circle. One makes a ground pass to one of his teammates while calling the name of the keeper to whom the ball must be played and moves into the position of the player receiving the pass. Duration: 2 minutes.

3. Four to five goalkeepers form a circle. One makes a ground pass to one of his teammates, playing a one-two with him at a close distance and going on in the same way with the other keepers. Duration: 2 minutes

Exercises to improve the technique of passing the ball back to the goalkeeper

1. Back pass to the goalkeeper, who controls the ball (two touches) and kicks the ball as far as possible.

2. Back pass to the goalkeeper who takes a long volley kick.

3. Bouncing back pass to the goalkeeper who takes a long volley kick.

4. The coach gives a back pass to the goalkeeper and shouts a number before the ball gets to the keeper. If he calls an uneven number, the keeper kicks the ball as far as possible; if he calls an even number, the keeper makes a diving save to catch the ball.

Exercises to enhance quick reflexes and speed of motion
Duration 25 minutes.

1. The coach is standing at a distance of about 6 yards from the goalkeeper and kicks two ground balls, calling them the white and the black

ball; when the two balls get into the goalkeeper's range of action, the coach shouts the color of the ball that the keeper has to catch (Variation: take mid-height shots).

2. The goalkeeper has his back to the coach, who is positioned between two balls - called ball no.1 and no.2 - and is holding a ball in his hands - called ball no.3. The coach throws the ball no.3 against the goal-keeper's shoulders and immediately calls the number of the ball that he has to intercept.

3. The goalkeeper is standing with his back to the coach, with his legs wide apart and a ball in his hands. He throws the ball through his legs to the coach (5 to 6 yards far from him), who takes a volley shot at goal immediately after the keeper has turned about to face him.

4. The goalkeeper is standing with a ball in his hands and his back to the coach. He throws the ball above his head to pass it to the coach, who takes a heading shot at goal.

Exercises to enhance quick reflexes and speed of motion by combining different saving actions
Duration: 12 minutes.

1. The coach throws the ball to the goalkeeper who is standing at the near post; immediately after catching the first ball the keeper rapidly lets it fall down to try to intercept a second ball kicked by the assistant coach (standing in the middle of the penalty box) at the far post. Variation: the assistant coach can throw a tennis ball.

2. The coach first takes a ground shot at goal and immediately after takes a mid-air shot always on the same side. Purpose of the exercise: favor an instant reaction to a situation characterized by a precarious coor-dination.

Exercise to improve high saving technique
The coach kicks a lobbed ball to the goalkeeper. Before catching the shot the keeper must turn around to see and shout the number that his teammate standing at the opposite post is showing with his fingers. Purpose of the exercise: practice high saving technique, stimulate careful observation (peripheral vision) and increase the speed of the last three steps preceding the take-off.

At the end of the exercise perform 3 minutes of stretching and some special exercises to release contraction of the back muscles.

Robin fell with a great splash into the brook